THE ANATOMY OF POPULAR
REBELLION IN THE MIDDLE AGES

Europe in the Middle Ages
Selected Studies

Volume 9

General Editor
RICHARD VAUGHAN
University of Hull

NORTH-HOLLAND PUBLISHING COMPANY – AMSTERDAM · NEW YORK · OXFORD

THE ANATOMY OF POPULAR REBELLION IN THE MIDDLE AGES

By
GUY FOURQUIN

Translated by
Anne Chesters

1978

NORTH-HOLLAND PUBLISHING COMPANY – AMSTERDAM · NEW YORK · OXFORD

Library of Congress Catalog Card Number: 77-22421
North-Holland ISBN: 0-444-85006-6

Published by:
North-Holland Publishing Company – Amsterdam/New York/Oxford

Distributors for the U.S.A. and Canada:
Elsevier North-Holland, Inc.
52, Vanderbilt Avenue, New York, N.Y. 10017

Library of Congress Cataloging in Publication Data
Fourquin, Guy.
    The anatomy of popular rebellion in the Middle Ages.

    (Europe in the Middle Ages; v. 9)
    Translation of Les soulèvements populaires au Moyen Age.
    Bibliography: p.
    1.   Social history—Medieval, 500–1500.
2. Social conflict. I. Title. II. Series.
HN11.F6813   309.1'02   77-22421
ISBN 0-444-85006-6

This book was originally published in French in 1972 under the title *Les soulèvements populaires au moyen âge*, Presses Universitaires de France, Paris

Printed in The Netherlands

General Editor's note

This suggestive and original work, which throws new light on the popular uprisings of the Middle Ages, was originally published as a paperback in 1972 with the title *Les soulèvements populaires au moyen âge*. The title chosen for the English translation is designed to emphasise that this is something more than a 'straight' history: it is a discussion, an analysis, of a wide-ranging and puzzling historical phenomenon. Mrs Chesters' text, which has been seen and approved by Professor Fourquin, has needed only the lightest revision by myself; the index is hers.

April 1977

Richard Vaughan
General Editor

Contents

Introduction

"An attitude of constant indignation is the sign of a great poverty of mind." *Paul Valéry*.

The term *rebellion* rather than *revolution* has been chosen deliberately because today's interpretation of the word 'revolution', which has undergone a change since the eighteenth century, is in no way suited to the Middle Ages, nor even to later periods. It took a long while for revolution to be spoken of in political or social spheres: Commynes was one of the first to use the phrase *revolutions des estats*. Later, in his *Leviathan*, Hobbes talks of the "revolution of states" by analogy with the 'revolution' of the planets. For a long time the term was used only in astronomy, or else to denote an immense upheaval in which the upper and lower poles changed places: during its revolution a planet moves from one point on its trajectory to another which is directly opposite. Thus, for Hobbes, revolution in a state is "a reversal of the given situation in which the inferior becomes superior and the superior inferior" (J. Monnerot). Previously, political philosophy – that of a Jean Bodin or a Machiavelli, for example – preferred to speak of *conjurations, seditions* or, like the Greeks, *insurrections* or *changes*. None of these terms in any way evokes the idea of turning and returning (old order – revolution – new order). Although Hobbes understood revolution in this way, this is not to say that he placed any hopes in it: for him it was simply the sign of the instability of human things, a reversal of situation which would not be final, since the wheel would continue turning. His was a cyclic conception of revolution, without value judgement. And up to the end of the eighteenth century, as far as political theory was concerned, revolution was simply a question of a reversal of situation, which was not presumed to be good in itself (and neither was its opposite presumed to be bad).

We have thus not yet reached the linear conception of history which was to divide it into a *before* (bad) and an *after* (necessarily good). Certainly, there were many millenarianisms in the Middle Ages which had a linear conception of evolution: an 'absolute beginning' was going to cut time in two, the *before* and *after*. But the word 'revolution' was never used by medieval eschatology, which was often the product of simple minds incapable of elaborating a complete political theory.

Everything changed with the 1789 Revolution, then with Marxism. From then on, the term carried with it a value judgement: the French Revolution and the revolution forecast by Marx were events which were good in themselves. And they did indeed cut time into two; the cyclic conception gave way to the linear conception. The Revolution (whose capital letter suggests an affinity with medieval allegories) is an act of complete change, a supreme and ultimate resort and a source of values. But attitudes to it have varied. At first and up to the beginning of the twentieth century, some men dared to look on it as the absolute evil, the "matrix of errors and aberrations"; they proclaimed themselves counter-revolutionaries. We have moved on from there and for the last half-century the word has nearly always been taken in good part: if one reacts against it, it is not to propose counter-revolution but another Revolution. There is here a complex psychological attitude which poses problems for the historian, just as anything which implies a value judgement poses problems for him.

Even if one wished to use the word, however, other difficulties would arise. J. Ellul notes that "a revolution implies a doctrine, a plan, a programme, some sort of theory". It is the "existence of this preliminary thinking which characterizes revolution". It is not enough to have insurgents, there must also be those whom A. Decouflé calls the *directors* of the revolution, in other words, organizers "who bring order after the storm has passed". Revolution supposes a definite beginning, "it has nothing to do with reforms, it is a starting from scratch". "The revolutionary plan is not concerned with applying an idealist doctrine", such as that of the millenarians, "nor with reforming some element or other of society; it is essentially concerned with the idea of a beginning .... Otherwise, the episode of unrest may be called social, political or tragic, but it cannot be called a revolution" (Ellul). The revolutionary proclaims the beginning of a totally new era in history, "a history never before recounted". All such things are distinctly foreign to the Middle Ages. Thus it was necessary to look for a different word: and so for our title we chose *rebellion* (in slight preference to revolt which is not entirely suitable for those movements where the elite is very much involved).

The title of this book includes the word 'popular' deliberately to limit the scope of the work, to eliminate those rebellions where the lower strata of society played practically no part. We have thus excluded movements which were either simply controlled by nobles or which offered them some hope of profit, such as those which preceded the signing of Magna Carta in the reign of King John or those which followed the death of Louis VIII when France was governed by a regency for the first time in her history. Instead we have concentrated on anything which can affect a fair range of social strata. But all the uprisings which have been kept were not *popular* to the same degree. The work would have been truncated if we had included only those revolts which were entirely popular, those where only the poor and people on the verge of poverty were involved – not the whole population which, as a body, can rise up only in *city-states*. And, in fact, one finds most frequently that numerous strata, very differently situated on the social ladder, have taken part in rebellions. Of these, we have preferred to concentrate on those where the lower orders have participated as agents or as a tactical force; closely involved with them one nearly always finds some of the upper strata (sometimes belonging to the elite, sometimes not).

The methodology adopted in the book, which is divided into two parts, 'Approaches to the Problem' and 'A Typology of the Rebellions' deserves some comment.

The Middle Ages have not been isolated from preceding or succeeding periods. Thus, in order to examine myths whose effect on the collective mentality is all too easily forgotten, we have made some incursions into ancient history and followed the progress of these myths up to the present day. But the most frequent references are to modern history: there is no intrinsic difference between medieval and modern rebellions. The millenarianism of the end of the Middle Ages finds a parallel in the Peasants' War in Luther's time; the peasant uprisings of the fourteenth century find an echo in those of the seventeenth century. The growth of the state as a source of social conflict is not merely a phenomenon of the modern period; it existed towards the end of the Middle Ages: both before and after 1500, the same causes have produced the same major effects.

There is no fixed equation: rebellion = social conflict arising from primarily economic causes. For there are no prime causes or series of causes 'in the last analysis'. In general, a rebellion is a fact of history in its entirety and, *a priori*, no branch of history should be ignored or under-estimated. Indeed, the historian of rebellion must not hesitate to call upon other disciplines which are concerned with collective mentalities, for example, social psychology and social mythology and notably those disciplines which deal with the *crowd*. Sociology, in particular, can render a very great service, not to mention ethnography, psychoanalysis . . . the list is lengthy.

Not so much because of the book's size, but more because in this interdisciplinary approach there is so much to be done in the medieval period, it has been possible only to touch lightly upon many aspects, and the book might thus give the reader the impression that it is just 'skimming' issues. But the risk has been knowingly run and more thorough studies will come later, studies which will depend not only on historians but also on specialists in many other indispensable disciplines. This book is an *attempt* to 'unlock' the history of rebellion in the Middle Ages in order to place medieval history more within reach of the modern cultured reader. In other words, it is an *open synthesis*.

PART I   APPROACHES TO THE PROBLEM

CHAPTER 1

The persistence of myths in the Middle Ages

We no longer believe that myths are, as the usual meaning of the term would seem to indicate, merely fables or inventions. Mircea Eliade, for example, has shown that the term also denotes a "true story" which is sacred, "exemplary and meaningful" and that this is so not only in primitive societies, but in more advanced cultures, in the Middle Ages and even, it seems, today. So myth is not purely and simply fiction; in most societies it is a living force, either constantly present or constantly renascent.

It is not only in very 'primitive' societies that prophetic cults announce the imminent approach of a marvellous era of abundance and beatitude. The Golden Age is a myth known to Antiquity and the Middle Ages, and there is no proof that it has been abandoned even by present-day societies. It is a myth which goes side by side with the "journey back to the origins" myth, itself closely linked to the prestige of 'beginnings'. Thus, many medieval chroniclers began their accounts with a description of the Creation. One may wonder why they deemed it necessary to go back to the Creation; it was because they felt, albeit subconsciously, the need for a periodic renewal of the world.

Myths before the Middle Ages

In the ancient Middle East this need for renewal was felt very strongly by the Egyptians, the Mesopotamians and the Israelites. In Eliade's terminology it is the "myth of the eternal return".

For the Mesopotamians, "the *beginning* was organically linked to an *end* which preceded it", an end which was of the same nature as the

3

'chaos' before the Creation and which was necessary for each new beginning; this idea is demonstrated clearly by their New Year rites. To the Egyptians, likewise, the New Year was symbolic of the Creation. The end was thus implicit in the beginning and vice versa: it is a notion which finds an echo in Machiavelli's *ritornar ai principi*. Now the passing of time implies "an increasing distance from the *beginnings*, . . . the loss of the initial perfection" of the Golden Age. Thus, "before something authentically new can begin, the remains and relics of the old cycle must be completely destroyed": since one cannot regenerate that which has degenerated, the old world must be destroyed so that it can be regenerated *in toto*. "The obsession with the blessedness of beginnings demands the complete destruction of everything that has existed since the Creation and yet is now debased: it is the only way to re-establish the initial perfection" (Eliade).

Belief in the excellence of beginnings has thus been projected into the future, a future sometimes timeless, sometimes imminent. The frequency of this belief in societies which are otherwise quite dissimilar from social, religious or intellectual points of view, explains the important role played in the history of mankind by the myth of the end of the world. Such a myth implies the 'unfixed nature' of the 'beginning': the origin is not only in a 'mythical' past, but in a more or less imaginary future. "This is the conclusion reached by the Stoics and Neo-Pythagoreans when elaborating systematically the idea of the eternal return. But the notion of the *origin* is linked, above all, to the idea of perfection and beatitude. This is why we find, in the conceptions of eschatology as a cosmogony of the future, the source of all those beliefs which proclaim the Golden Age, not only (or no longer) in the past, but also (or only) in the future" (Eliade).

Present-day societies have difficulty in understanding the optimism of such an eschatology because of their fears of a catastrophic end to the world through a nuclear explosion. For many of our contemporaries, in direct contrast with tribal societies or the ancients of the Middle East, the end will be radical and absolute; it will not be followed by any new creation of the world. Yet, thinking of the destruction of artistic language, plastic or otherwise, in the arts today (for example, the plays of Ionesco), one may wonder whether the writer or artist, in wishing to make a clean sweep of all previous literature, all previous art, in wishing to "go back to the beginning", is not embarking on a complex process, consciously or not, which will ultimately lead to the creation of a new universe. This is all the more possible since myths, variously camouflaged, have survived till today.

It is not only in the arts that modern revolutionary eschatology draws its inspiration from the predictions of Antiquity. In social history, the "Apocalypse fanatics" – as N. Cohn calls them – have played an important role from Hebrew times up to the present day, and not just in the Middle Ages steeped as they were in the Old Testament.

According to the Hebrews, God had charged Israel with "spreading light among the gentiles" and carrying salvation to the ends of the earth. A people chosen by Yahweh, the Israelites faced misfortune and oppression with the certainty of ultimate triumph. The Old Testament prophets speak of the immense cosmic catastrophe from which "there will arise a Palestine which will be nothing less than a new Eden, Paradise regained". Through its sins, the chosen people would bring about the Day of Yahweh, a Day of Wrath. Only the chosen few with unbroken faith would survive. As the instrument of God, the people thus purified and regenerated would see the Deliverer settle in Palestine in the midst of the Righteous. Jerusalem would be rebuilt. Zion would be the spiritual capital of the world which would be "a just world where the poor are protected, and a harmonious and peaceful world . . .". Of these 'apocalyptic' texts (Cohn's adjective is well-chosen, the Apocalypse being the revelation of that which was hidden), the most impressive is the dream of the prophet Daniel.

It was easy to strip these prophecies of their mystical meaning and invest them with a mythical sense while the old myths lived on (albeit clandestinely). They could also be used to form the central theme of 'revolutionary' eschatology in which the end of the world myth reappears time and again. Zoroastrian Iran exerted a major influence here: as elsewhere in the East, the myth of a passage from one world to another was very much alive. And Iranian religion stated unequivocally that the new world would be the exact opposite of its predecessor, the one being overturned by the other (note the etymology of the word 'revolution'). There must be a long period of waiting before the terrible trials which will lead to the ultimate victory of Good. "And it is this *long period of waiting* which will form the basis of *chiliasm* or *millenarianism*, the thousand years indicating not a precise point in time but, quite the contrary, the vast expanse of time which will elapse before the *great event*. The number thousand is a fatidic one for signalling the end of time. But the Day will come, a Day which will be unlike any other and which, later, will serve as a means of dividing time into a *before* and an *after*. The concept of this *absolute beginning* which follows an *absolute end*, itself preceded by a *long period of waiting*, is fundamental" (J. Monnerot). The term Apocalypse thus gains a new dimension: more than just a prophecy of mysterious happenings, it heralds the end of the world, the new distribution of beings and objects, an end which is only a beginning.

Eschatology and apocalyptism are linked with messianism. Redemption through the coming of a *kingdom* heralded by a Saviour (a belief found throughout history perhaps – even amongst pagans) is one of the most fundamental religious principles of Zoroaster's faith. But if we use the term 'messianism' to indicate belief in the coming of a Saviour it is, of course, because the Old Testament, after the exile in Babylon, called Him *the anointed one*, hence *Messiah*. Later, some will maintain that the Antichrist must come before the Messiah, following the belief of Iranian paganism that Evil must precede Good. In any event, excess of evil shows how near is the coming of Good, the advent of the Messiah.

The Hebrews then, as a whole, were not always able to dissociate themselves from the mixture of myth and fancy which are essentially pagan characteristics. To the Hebrews, the universe seemed dominated by some evil power whose tyranny constantly aggravated the sufferings of its victims. But the hour would come when the saints would stand up and fight. It would be the apogee of history and the saints would take over the leadership from the defeated tyrant: this kingdom of saints which, in its brilliance, would eclipse all previous kingdoms, would have no successor since it would be at once a beginning and an end.

At the time of the Roman occupation, messianic dreams were a stimulus for the Jews. But the Jewish conception of the Messiah had evolved. If for the prophets – as for the disciples of the New Testament – the Saviour was God himself, some Jews later saw him quite simply as a monarch, though a very wise and powerful one. Then, in the first century BC, for example in the Apocalypses of Baruch and Ezra, he was seen as a superhuman warrior with miraculous powers. The historian Josephus was probably correct in thinking that it was through their belief that the coming of their messianic king was at hand that the Jews launched themselves into the 'suicide-war' which ended in 70 AD with the destruction of the Temple. It is here that the Jews' apocalyptic faith died.

The messianic prophecies were then adopted by the Christians: to a certain extent, compensatory visions of the future are nurtured so that those who are oppressed are better able to bear the present. From Nero onwards, Christians have used and even distorted the Apocalypse of St John in proclaiming their faith in the imminence of the age of the Messiah during which all persecutors will be overthrown. The millennium will only end with the resurrection of the dead and the Last Judgement. From the second century this idea found vigorous expression in Montanism, which believed that the second coming of Christ was imminent since St John had said it would come to pass 'shortly'. Yet those Christians who were not visionaries recalled that the second epistle of St Peter did not declare the return of Christ to be imminent. Neither did all Christians believe that at the end of the world the saints would live for a thousand years in a new Jerusalem. Even so, there were others who had an almost materialistic conception of the kingdom of saints: for them it would be essentially the Golden Age of the pagans, a time of material abundance rather than spiritual perfection.

The idea of a millennium, whether Christian or tinged with paganism, came to Gaul at the end of the first century with the coming to Lyons of Bishop Irenaeus. His great work, *Against heresies*, is "a comprehensive anthology of the messianic and millenarian prophecies culled from the Old and New Testaments", but also includes those in the writings of the Phrygian, Papias, who had attributed to Christ somewhat spurious millenarian prophecies inspired by Judaic writings. Thus the "compensatory phantasies" send Bishop Irenaeus, faced with the trials and tribulations of his time, along the same path as the Jews. And, in the fourth century, in order to convert the Jews, Lactantius could think of nothing better than to extol the attractions of the millennium to them. In the fifth century Commodianus went further and the men of the Middle Ages were not to forget his threatening 'prophecies'; for him more than for his predecessors, vengeance and victory were inseparable. So Christ would not return accompanied by the angels, but at the head of the descendants of the ten lost tribes of Israel, gathered from the forgotten corners of the earth. These saints, although not knowing hatred, would, for all that, be none the less warriors. Antichrist would be put to flight. His troops would become enslaved under the yoke of the Holy People who, having gained eternal youth, would live for ever in a Holy Jerusalem, freed of all evil and endowed with all earthly goods. This is something which many insurgents in the Middle Ages were not to forget and which twentieth-century totalitarian doctrines have taken up again: domination by the *poor* is domination by the good of the bad, just as the victory of the Righteous is their domination of the wicked.

The Fathers of the Church and other Christian authors of the end of Antiquity and the beginning of the Middle Ages rejected this Utopian idea. Even in the third century, Origen had written that the coming of the kingdom would be neither in space nor time but in the souls of Christians. And on reading St Augustine we see that the Church was increasingly anxious to 'keep its distance' with regard to chiliastic theories. Nothing could be further removed from the myth than his *City of God*, in which he states that the Apocalypse of St John should be interpreted only as a spiritual allegory, the birth of Christianity and the founding of the Church having already signalled the advent of the millennium. And in 431 the Ecumenical Council at Ephesus, in perfect agreement with Augustinian thought, condemned as superstition belief in a future millennium: the theologians had understood the danger posed by an ancient myth which, though disguised, persisted still.

Myths during the Middle Ages

Despite being condemned by the Church, the myth of a coming millennium was going to live on "in the obscure underworld of popular religion" (Cohn): its persistence is one of those pagan or semi-pagan traits which evangelization will not always succeed in stamping out.

Beliefs in the millennium supported the idea (originally Jewish) of a chosen people who, depending on the time and circumstances, were sometimes the whole of the Christian following or sometimes – and this was serious from a social point of view – just a group of Christians. Such beliefs held a real fascination for the people, particularly the oppressed, the rootless or unbalanced, and this fascination was, of course, greatly heightened during periods of unrest. Each troubled age turned to the Apocalypse and, even more, to a series of apocalyptic writings, the 'Sibylline Oracles' of the Middle Ages which were inspired by Hellenistic Judaism. Thus it is that two figures had a lasting fascination for the popular mentality – Antichrist and the Emperor of the Last Days. The long reign of the Emperor would be an era of abundance and would see the ultimate triumph of Christianity, with heathens having to choose between baptism and death. Overshadowing somewhat the image of Christ, the image of the Emperor conjured up a vision of the Golden Age and the violence necessary to attain it. But after his reign, Antichrist would set up his throne in the Temple at Jerusalem; he would deceive the multitude with his miracles and the Righteous, refusing to be duped, would be persecuted. Fortunately, the Lord would cut short this hateful reign by sending St Michael to overthrow Antichrist. Then would come to pass the second advent of God which would thus have been preceded by two brutal reigns, first Good then Evil.

Throughout the Middle Ages man was fascinated by the figure of Antichrist which he confused with the Dragon of the bowels of the Earth, with Satan. This Satan–Antichrist figure was for him "a gigantic embodiment of anarchic, destructive power". And it was not merely love of insult which, in the thirteenth century, prompted Innocent IV and Frederick II, for example, to call each other Antichrist or, three centuries later, for the pope to be called thus by the Protestants.

People were thus almost constantly watching for signs which would announce the coming of the Emperor or Antichrist, full of hopes and fears that find an echo in so many medieval chronicles. And politics became involved. Men strove to discover signs heralding harmony amongst Christians, victory over the ungodly and the unparalleled plenty and prosperity which would characterize the Golden Age. More than one king, on his accession, saw himself likened to the Last Emperor, hence the messianic titles which were bestowed on him, *the new David, rex justus* . . . . Then, when disillusion came, the beginning of the Golden Age was deferred until the following reign. More than one prince let himself be thought of as at least the precursor who was to open the way for the Last Emperor. These were fallacious hopes, but so strong that, like the Byzantine emperors, some sovereigns of France or Germany occasionally yielded to temptation and looked to the prophecies of the Sibylline Books to justify some or other claim to supreme power. But at the same time, a watch was kept for signs announcing the pain and miseries which would come with Antichrist. These signs were numerous: war, civil discord, plague, famine, natural catastrophies (serious drought, floods, severe winters), the sighting of comets, birth of monsters, and bad rulers. Invasions and the approach of the Saracens, Huns or Magyars, Mongols or Turks were readily interpreted as the coming of the hordes of Antichrist, the peoples of Gog and Magog. More often, a wicked lord or an unjust or brutal prince was likened to Antichrist and would be given the same names, most frequently *rex iniquus*. Then, with the passing of time, he would be considered merely the precursor of the Dragon. As can be seen, this myth or collection of closely interwoven myths lent themselves admirably to political or social exploitation: the "contiguity of extremes", as Monnerot calls it, the intimate connection between the violence of war and the radiant light of the new Jerusalem, was one of the most significant features in the history of medieval mentality, to say nothing of that of subsequent generations.

Christian orthodoxy has not then always enjoyed undivided

supremacy over the collective mentality, particularly during periods of
unrest and amongst peoples or social categories who were "a prey to
history", those whose very survival was threatened, or who at least
believed it to be so. But "the apocalyptic imagination, the way in which it
conceives of a future beginning which will follow an end, is closely
connected to the way in which it conceives present evils (evils for which
the new beginning will more than compensate). And it is on *earth* that all
things come to pass . . .. It is the coming on *earth* of the Kingdom of
Heaven that is awaited." "And as it is on earth that all things come to
pass, the Saviour who is to come after [the present turmoil] will use the
same terrestrial weapons as the enemy. He will be the *Lord of the Sword*.
Such representations are virtually heretical, everything about them being
immanent, materialistic and non-allegoric. [There was] something of a
tendency to take everything literally. Instead of conceiving of the
Evangelical Christ, people imagined an Anti-Genghis-Khan. It is myths
which provide a framework for one's perception of history. People
'recognize' what has been prophesied in what is happening . . ."
(Monnerot).

   In talking of collective mentalities one inevitably moves into the field
of psychoanalysis, since all societies raise the problem of individual and
collective origins. Freud saw clearly that psychoanalysis, unlike the other
sciences of life, culminates in the idea that the 'beginnings' of each human
being constitute a sort of Paradise. Everyone is tempted to transpose this
idea – which is false in itself – on to a social plane. But that is not all: the
myths which we have just considered also have a psychical content, and
psychoanalysts are inclined to see in the vision of the world which the
Middle Ages, for example, had, a mortal struggle between good fathers
and sons on the one hand and wicked fathers and sons on the other.
Certainly this crude notion is evident in the figures cherished by popular
eschatology and thus in the 'mass' movements which drew their
inspiration and great strength from them, as well as their 'fervour'. The
Emperor of the Last Days, and Christ too, is for some groups *at once* the
image of the ideal father, wise, just and protector of the weak, and that of
the good son who will radically change the world. The eschatological
leader – and there will be many such in the Middle Ages – is both
superhumanly powerful and always victorious: his armies can march only
to victory; justice and abundance can know no limits. This is a fanciful
representation which is liable to be projected on to a living person who
will be seen by his faithful followers and sons as possessing great powers,
including the power of working miracles. His army will be the army of the
saints against whom will rise up the demoniac fathers and sons.

Contemporary accounts of medieval eschatological 'fervours' liked to stress the eloquence of the 'messiahs of the poor', and the fascination which even they had for their 'electrified' followers, a fascination and fanaticism which look forward surprisingly to certain features of Nazism, for example. If several of these 'messiahs' were impostors, others certainly – and very probably the majority – sincerely believed themselves to be messiahs who would regenerate the world and rid it of wicked men; their belief was easily communicated to the multitude awaiting the eschatological Saviour. But for the eruption of a 'fervour' it needed particularly favourable circumstances: a situation contrasting greatly with the drabness of everyday experience, and perils which were new and therefore strange. Yet it is not certain that a general disorder was necessarily the impetus in all cases.

The Church has often – but not always, at least at first – considered these movements to be waves of heresy. The history of heresies, like that of myths or psychoanalysis, is to an extent inseparable from the history of popular rebellions. Some heretics thought of themselves quite complacently as the ten righteous capable of saving Sodom after the rout of the wicked. Common to all medieval heresies are certain features which have given rise either to insurrections or at least to the use of violence; through their prophet-leaders all these heresies refuse to accept any longer Christian orthodoxy concerning the consequences of original sin. The loss of the original state of innocence, as propounded by the Stoic, Posidonius, had brought with it the loss of what Engels was to call "primitive communism": it was then that the repressive instruments of society were born (the appearance of the State, of the power of man over man and of law over man); it was then, too, that one saw the beginnings of individual ownership. These ideas reappear in other Ancients, such as Cicero and Seneca, and not surprisingly since, in a rather confused way, they are extensions of the myths of the purity of beginnings and the Golden Age. However, and in this they are precursors of Christianity to a certain extent, the Stoics believed, if not in original sin, at least in the fall. It goes without saying that these points of view have been modified by Christian orthodoxy since; for the Fathers of the Church, all the restraint imposed on the individual by power, private property, the dependence of some on others (for example, slavery), in short all political, economic or social institutions, have a *corrective* value. Without, of course, being able to blot out original sin, they lessen its harmful consequences: the state of innocence was lost with the fall of Adam, but order, however imperfect, is preferable to disorder. Human institutions are inevitably imperfect, but they are necessary. This is precisely what many medieval heresies rejected, always under the influence of myths which they more or less subconsciously used to their own ends.

It is not without justification that medieval heresies have been compared to the ideologies which have supplanted them over the last two hundred years or so. Like ideology – as it was understood in the nineteenth century – heresy represents a kind of 'clinical symptom': it is a deviation, a 'bending' in a precise direction of one part (always the same) of Christian doctrinal patrimony. Etymologically, the word 'heresy' has the same meaning as the word 'choice'. Like heresy, ideology is the result of a choice: "psychological pressure . . . culminates in the choosing of certain psychical elements and arranging or combining them in such a way as to form an ideology". This happens, not because of a need for truth, but because of the demands of the emotions.

Medieval heresies are often eschatological: Good will soon succeed Evil, the last will be first. As such, they are both messianic (the prophet whose teachings one follows is the precursor of the Saviour or the Saviour himself) and violent since the Saviour is a Saviour of the Sword. And they are headed by an 'elite of redeemers' who seduce the people and act sooner or later as if they were not bound by the consequences of original sin. This elite is convinced that it is 'in a state of natural innocence', which is quite heretical since a return to nature would be for the Church a return to sin without Christ's redemption. These heresiarchs were optimists, fore-runners of Jean Jacques Rousseau: freed from the teachings of the Church they trusted only in their own 'virtue'. The consequences of this are enormous, because this confidence in one's own virtue, as we see in child psychology, goes hand in hand with a conviction of others' blameworthiness: violence is the logical result of these two convictions. Undoubtedly, the violence instigated by certain medieval heresies and even certain *crowd* movements which were not heretical (but which were motivated by the same crude psychology) can be compared with the outbursts of revolutionary violence in the modern era: in England, the Great Rebellion and, an even better example, the French Revolution. Robespierre would say that "his conscience was on his side"; the executions of the Reign of Terror seemed to him to stem simply from a "virtuous impatience".

In all these movements, which can legitimately be called sectarian in the full sense of the word, the necessary extermination of the Wicked before the coming of the Righteous is, in principle, carried out because the exterminators are certain that their actions are consistent with the values which they proclaim to the world: their ideology interprets present suffering in apocalyptic terms, even if there is no longer any reference to the Bible (as has been the case, in fact, since the French Revolution). And since, in the Middle Ages, rebellion was usually followed by brutal repression, the new sufferings which resulted were, in their turn, interpreted in apocalyptic terms. The same is true again later with, for example, the rebellion of the Anabaptists.

The historical continuity of heretical and sectarian uprisings in the Middle Ages and later cannot be denied. It is just as if a 'model' had passed from one generation to the next, and the features which go to make up this model are: "millenarianism, primitivism, secularism (everything happens on earth), eschatology, violence, messianism, pathological infatuation (anyone who does not think like me does not deserve to live), metaphysical optimism (all ends well) and moral optimism (I am good), anti-asceticism, collectivism or communism (which is an inherent characteristic of the innocent mind: to possess something is to lose everything)" (Monnerot). Everything happens down here; man does not go up to Heaven, it is Heaven that comes down. This is no different from what any 'contestatory' movement claims today, and religion has now become scarcely more than a process of temporal 'liberation' of men, a process of 'struggle' which is breaking down the present-day structures of society.

It is worth while looking at the survival of these myths and the ways of thinking which are bound up with them even today. All this surely had an influence, probably subconscious, on historians of popular rebellions. In any event, the egalitarian demands of medieval sects have been recognized as existing during the period of unrest which preceded, accompanied and followed the 1789 Revolution. They had, admittedly, become secular demands, but this secularization was quite consistent with that secularism which first saw light in the Middle Ages: Heaven had completed its descent to Earth. Completely stripped of its apparently Christian trappings, this myth has come to life again in the various revolutions of the nineteenth and twentieth centuries, as well as in socialist (including communist) doctrines.

CHAPTER 2

The sociology and history of rebellions

A product of the nineteenth century, sociology is to a great extent the creation of Saint-Simon and Auguste Comte. The somewhat idyllic vision, influenced as it was by Romanticism, which they had of the Middle Ages has weighed heavily on the works of their successors in that they have felt obliged to contradict the original theories. This is the case particularly with the Marxists.

The Middle Ages as seen by the nineteenth century

Although for both Saint-Simon and Auguste Comte temporal power was essentially power of a military nature in the Middle Ages – which is a fairly accurate assumption – neither of them considered that the role of violence in history could explain everything. On the contrary, for them, the system which they call feudal answered perfectly respectable needs.

It was quite different for Marx and Engels. In opposition to Dühring for whom "violence is the absolute evil", Engels in his *Anti-Dühring* puts forward quite clearly the Marxist position: "Violence plays . . . in history . . . a revolutionary role; . . . it is the midwife of every old society which is pregnant with the new, . . . it (is) the instrument by the aid of which social movement forces its way through and shatters the dead, fossilized, political forms . . . . All political violence is originally based on an economic, social function, and increases in proportion as the members of society, through the dissolution of the primitive community [an allusion to primitive communism], become transformed into private producers."

The idea of the determinant strength of the economic infrastructure,

15

which is fundamental to Marxism, is repeated time and time again in the writings of Marx and Engels. It is from this that the expression 'historical materialism' developed, an expression which Marx did not use (the term is Kautsky's) but one which he would not have rejected. Although Marx's ideas were not always constant the point remains that for him economic factors determine – or, perhaps, condition – political, religious and intellectual superstructures. Thus, and the founders of Marxism have said it again and again, popular rebellions are motivated by fundamentally economic factors.

It was in Saint-Simon that Marx came across the idea of the 'advent' of an economic era, particularly in the Parable of the Talents: the age of warriors and priests had come to an end, that of *industrialists*, bankers and scientists was beginning. The predominance of the economy has as its corollary the social supremacy of the men who manage the economy. Comtism had maintained much the same. Karl Marx adopts the idea but 'bends' it. For in the eyes of his predecessors, this dominant power of the economy was an innovation of the nineteenth century; and what is more, it would be manifest only in the future (albeit the near future) *not* in the past. On the other hand, Marx who, like many of his contemporaries, believed excessively in the 'laws of nature', thought that the domination of the economic infrastructure over the superstructures and the pre-eminence of the 'industrialists' (in the Saint-Simonian sense) over other men are just as much retrospective as prospective: this pre-eminence does not herald the dawn of new eras, it characterizes all the past history of mankind. It is pointless, then, to seek non-economic primary causes for any popular rebellion in any age. *The German ideology* is an excellent illustration of this thesis.

Primacy of the economy implies primacy of production. The differences which exist between human societies are precisely the differences in their methods of production; this has always been the case, no matter where. The social importance of one category of men and its place on the social ladder are a function of the relationship between that category and production. Thus there are social classes and consequently class conflict. The determining factor of the division into classes is the exploitation of the work of one section by another: "The specific form whereby unpaid surplus-labour is extracted from the immediate producer determines the domination–subjection relationship." This is one of the clearest formulae found in *Capital*, and the idea, when not stated explicitly, is implicit in the entire works of Marx and Engels. Every society is divided into the exploiters and the exploited; any historical situation can be explained by this division which is one of intense opposition between two social categories or classes. *The Communist manifesto* sets this out clearly: "The history of all hitherto existing society is the history of class struggles. Freeman and slave, patrician and plebeian, lord and serf, guild-master [but some were surely rather poor] and journeyman, in a word, oppressor and oppressed, stood in constant opposition to one another, carried on an uninterrupted, now hidden, now open fight that each time ended, either in a revolutionary reconstitution of society at large, or in the common ruin of the contending classes."

The criterion which governs this "polarized concept of human society" (Monnerot) is the existence of the right of ownership. Indeed for Marx, property determines authority and dominance and he sees this as true of any historical period. One is an exploiter if one has the tools for manufacturing, and exploited – therefore deprived – if one has not. All ownership is thus deprivation, and one thinks of Jean Jacques Rousseau and especially Proudhon for whom "property is theft". If there are both rich and poor it is because the former have robbed the latter. Since ownership of the means of production necessarily makes the owners all-powerful, they dominate the non-owners in every sense (including the political): the exploitation of man by man can therefore end only with the abolition of private ownership.

In fact, private ownership has the same place and function in Marxism as original sin in Christianity. Marx has formulated a general category from one precise, scandalous fact: the exploitation of the English proletariat of his time by the Manchester industrialists. Except in 'primitive' communism – whose existence remains to be proved – and socialism in its ultimate form, property, the absolute evil, is dominant; indeed, Monnerot has asked whether property might not be the archetypal symbol of a "time of trial and suffering situated half-way between two symmetrical paradises". This would then bring sociology back to an examination of medieval myths. We recall that for the Fathers of the Church and medieval theologians, *dominium* (private ownership *and* political power) was the consequence of original sin, but a 'corrective' consequence. For Marx, on the other hand, property is indeed the absolute Evil against which one must revolt: human nature is in no way corrupt and when man has got rid of this alienating force, property, he will have restored human essence which, for the Marxists like Rousseau, is 'good'.

Present-day problems in the sociology of conflict

It is especially necessary to understand the Marxist position, since it
influences many sociologists and historians. Yet many objections have
been made to what is in some respects a sort of 'theodicy', notably by
sociologists who do not accept without question the elements of truth
which it may at first sight contain.

   We refer to that branch of sociology which deals with 'social change'.
The question it has to ask itself is whether this 'social change' (a somewhat
vague term) can be explained by just one, or several, dominant factors.
This has led to an extremely important debate which has brought into
conflict several schools of thought and which has crystallized around one
central issue: should more weight be given to things rather than ideas, to
material rather than non-material conditions, to structural factors rather
than cultural? This conflict is highlighted by the opposition between the
intellectualist concept of history – as in Auguste Comte – and the
materialist concept – as in Marx. But at the moment sociology seems to
be leaning towards a relativist point of view: even those who put the
stress on one particular factor generally recognize that social change is
always the result of a plurality of causes which act simultaneously and
react one against the other.

   From the beginning, sociology had been interested in *change*: this is
true of Comte for whom dynamic sociology (studying progress, namely
the transformation of societies) was more important than a static
sociology devoted to the study of order; it is even more true of Marx,
some of whose followers have gone so far as to suggest that sociology
should study society primarily, if not exclusively, from the point of view of
the changes that take place within it. Today there is an upsurge of interest
in the study of change, not only because of the crises in modern-day
'advanced' societies and the Third World, but also because a more open
welcome is being accorded to the works of Marx, now recognized not just
as a philosopher or prophet, but also as a sociologist. Now Marx put the
accent, as one might expect, on the sociology of conflict. And rightly so,
even if one disagrees with Marxist conclusions.

   Ralf Dahrendorf has undertaken a close analysis of Marx's sociology
as well as the sociology of his followers and his critics. According to this
German-born sociologist, Marx makes an important contribution to the
sociology of conflict. But Marx made three mistakes. He reduced all
major social conflicts to class struggles; but class, even when it exists, is

just one of the interest groups which bring into opposition the members of a society. His second mistake was to insist that the struggle between the classes leads inevitably to revolution, in other words, that all social conflict ends in a violent solution and revolution is the only dynamic moment in history. But a violent *solution* is, in the Middle Ages as at other times, the exception, and compromise (or evolution) the rule: the dominant social group makes various concessions and even goes as far as to borrow some new idea from the rioters or insurgents. Throughout history the dominant groups, as is too frequently forgotten, have rarely been overthrown. Finally, Marx's third mistake: for him the origin of conflict lies in the ownership of the means of production, whereas it is the control of these means which matters much more than their ownership.

Dahrendorf's own theory of conflict is less interesting to medievalists since his analyses bear on more recent periods. His central idea, however, is of interest to them: according to him it is not enough to explain social conflict purely in psychological terms, as if it were simply the result of a build-up of personal feelings or emotions – which is nevertheless true of certain medieval uprisings; instead, one has to discover the permanent source which provokes and nourishes conflicts within the structure and method of functioning of social organization – which is not always the case in medieval times. Now the major structural source of social conflict lies not in the unequal division of property but in the unequal distribution of authority between men. For Dahrendorf, who follows Max Weber here, authority is the "probability that a command with a given specific content will be obeyed by a given group of persons". Authority is thus distinct from power which is the "probability that one actor within a social relationship will be in a position to carry out his own will despite resistance". And there is a 'dichotomy' in the distribution of authority: a few share it amongst themselves while everyone else goes without (with wealth on the other hand, some simply have more than others, nobody being completely without, even tramps). There is thus a clash of interest between two groups, the one which commands and the one which obeys; it is from this that the permanent nature of conflict comes about: the confrontation is not between classes but between interest groups. It is these groups and their attitudes which determine the intensity and violence of the conflict. The intensity and violence both decline, for example, when the interest groups have been able to organize themselves, when the distribution of authority does not coincide with the distribution of other economic and social advantages, when the parties concerned realize what separates them and do not inveigh against each other and when each one does not consider its opponent to be the incarnation of evil.

Dahrendorf's thinking is particularly perceptive in one area. As a sociologist of conflict he realizes, unlike the Marxists, that society is not merely a system in conflict but that at the same time it is an integrated system. It is precisely because authority is an integrating factor that it is at the same time a factor of conflict. Dahrendorf has however been criticized. In Guy Rocher's view, for example, the conflict of interests cannot, any more than 'class' conflict, account for all the facts of social change. One may wonder, moreover, whether there are always two sides in simple opposition as Dahrendorf (quite close to Marx on this point) would have it. The domination–subjection relationship may be less clearly defined. And is it really certain that there are no gradations in authority as there are in wealth? Guy Rocher points out, too, that there can be contradictions within the structures of society, contradictions which are in no way a product of simple production relationships, as the Marxists would see it, but a product of history: "Just as geological strata lie one on top of the other . . ., in society older institutions coexist with more recent ones" – a fairly ordinary observation for a historian but less usual for a sociologist. We can look at two examples from the Middle Ages: laws of different eras were able to coexist (such as feudal law and the laws of the bourgeoisie and the towns); new professions and organizations were able to appear without the old ones disappearing (for example, the various urban working communities which grew up between the eleventh and fifteenth centuries). *Generations* of social institutions and practices coexist, but the old and the new cannot always live together without the growth of tension and conflict.

The distinction between revolt and revolution

Contemporary sociology is little disposed to make the distinction between rebellion or revolt and revolution; it must be remembered, however, that the men of the Middle Ages were sometimes insurgents but they were never revolutionaries. The difficulty of distinguishing clearly between the two phenomena, revolt and revolution, has been recently stressed by Jacques Ellul: this "differentiation between revolt and revolution when one considers them in history rather than in the abstract is (moreover) difficult and uncertain". In opposition to Albert Camus, who not so long ago established a distinction between metaphysical revolt and historical revolt, Ellul maintains that "there is *only* historical revolt" for it alone results in "a process of questioning which in turn will perhaps make it possible to discover the trace of an answer in an attitude of man towards life". And in any revolt there are two constant features, a belief that one is faced with the intolerable and an act of accusation. A man or a collectivity revolts when "an act, a situation or a relationship reaches the intolerable (injustice, poverty, starvation, oppression, indignity)". Man thus revolts because it is impossible to carry on any longer. But it is not a question of feeling, and social psychology and psychoanalysis do not give a complete explanation according to Ellul who notes, moreover, that it is quite unproductive, if not futile, to look for an explanation or cause of a revolt in the psychological make-up of the chief insurgent.

If we speak of *liberty* in connection with revolt we should remember what sociologists frequently do not, that "the meaning is corrupted by our experience of history". If it has become for us a "subject of philosophy or political science", it had, before the eighteenth century, "a different import, directly relevant to man's everyday existence". It used to be that man's wish was to escape a destiny which had become intolerable and the struggle against the oppressor was only "secondary, indirect". Whilst revolution always sees itself as 'constructive' and claims that it will lead to a brighter tomorrow, revolt is a "titanic rebellion causing things to break up and having no foreseeable future". Whereas revolution is always an act filled with hope, "revolt has despair at its heart"; was it not one of the Florentine leaders of the Revolt of the Ciompi who exclaimed: "Everywhere where fear of hunger and prison exists, as it does amongst us, there can be no room for fear of Hell"?

The man in revolt has thus had enough of the times through which he has lived; and in some ways it is possible to say that "revolt is both reactionary and illuminist". We ought to get back to the good old days, say the insurgents, even those not imbued with a messianic spirit; we ought to be governed according to the old ways, say so many insurgents in the Middle Ages and the seventeenth century. As they often cannot see any possible future, as the future in fact could only be a worsening of this present existence of which they have had enough, there comes a time when the insurgents are overcome by passivity, either when the rebellion breaks down, or even while it is temporarily on the ascendant. And yet, and this is apparently contradictory, as a result of a search for compensation, almost all revolts lead sooner or later towards illuminism:

"Man responds to an excess of suffering by revolt and by steeping himself at the same time in myth" (Ellul). This is why revolt was often to result only in a void until myth underwent the changes which the nineteenth and twentieth centuries forced on it, finally giving it real strength. Neither medieval nor modern revolts have been able to alter historical reality even when their reasons and objectives were legitimate, even when they were temporarily successful. "The future of a sedition on the one hand, and its motives and objectives on the other, are very different things" (R. Mousnier). The sight of an enemy to overthrow is too immediate, as is the poverty which must be fought against, and no one has shown himself capable of solidly uniting regions which revolt at the same time: compare the revolt of Spartacus in Antiquity, the peasant revolts towards the end of the Middle Ages or the revolt of Thomas Münzer in the Germany of the Reformation. Mousnier's statement concerning the insurgents of the seventeenth century, that "these peasants were violently angry men but not revolutionaries, ... (that) their outburst was not an attempt at revolution", finds an echo in Ellul who notes that "revolt is in no way a minor revolution or an unsuccessful one" since the two belong to "different categories".

In general the insurgent gains nothing from victory: "victor or vanquished, the insurgent can only draw nearer death" (Ellul) because death seems preferable to him than life. Of course, during the insurrection, numerous objectives may take shape, but they vary: an agent of the royal or princely exchequer is set upon or a strong room plundered; then, with the revolt feeding on itself for some time, there can be a change of direction with leaders on the spot proposing different actions, but always immediate ones. Next comes repression: the revolt may then re-erupt – something which is more common in the modern period than in the Middle Ages – and find its second wind. One demand may be that the 'demonstrators' who have been arrested should be freed. On the other hand, should those in power (whose authority is not always under debate) make concessions, the revolt will flare up again and demand further concessions. Here too, on the whole, there are relatively few medieval examples except in the towns.

Finally, revolt is never *for*; by its very essence it is *against*. It is notably against progress, and the Lyons revolt of 1832 came after a long succession of revolts hostile to technical innovations. The fear of unemployment, which was looked upon as an invention of the devil, provoked rebellion against the new machines; the *Ongles bleus* rebelled against the new weaving-looms, and in the fifteenth century others rebelled against rival techniques in silk-manufacturing. Other 'innovations' likewise caused violent reactions, and at the end of the Middle Ages people frequently rose against the fiscal powers of the kings or princes, powers which came into being, depending on the region, during the thirteenth or fourteenth centuries. This was true from Scandinavia to Aragon, taking in England, the Empire and France. But what was the main reason for revolt? Was it the weight of taxation, the presence of fiscal agents who were often strangers to the area, or was it the principle of taxation itself? It depends on the specific circumstances, but what is certain is that revolt is in all such cases a rejection of a distant and developing power.

For Ellul, the sense of the intolerable, which we have just examined, includes within it the idea of accusation. The insurgent accuses the Other, a 'someone' whose identity is at times left in a strange obscurity. The accused are *They*, the men responsible for a situation which has become intolerable and which is felt to be so. But sooner or later a face must be given to these scapegoats. "The more clearly the insurgent sees the apocalypse of his objectives, the more specific he is in his accusation." Or, at least, he thinks he is since he ends by transposing the face of the accused into the features of someone near: in the seventeenth century, according to Mousnier, and even before the end of the Middle Ages, the indeterminate enemy is the state, but one ends by identifying it with the form of its nearest agent, even if he be only a very subordinate officer. The king or prince is very rarely attacked, but his regional representative is set upon quite readily.

It is fashionable today amongst many historians and sociologists to interpret everything in terms of class conflict, but the insurgent takes little notice of 'class' – always supposing it exists – or even of social strata. This is so to the extent that there operates between very different social groups a 'vertical solidarity' which emerges during revolts and amongst insurgents when there is general ferment. In other words, social inequality was not necessarily the cause of the traditional revolts which came before the end of the eighteenth century. And the notion of liberty in these revolts did not have the wider meaning which we are accustomed to give it today and which is current among sociologists: liberty was then a struggle against taxation as such and against the agents of the state as such, whoever they might be. It is curious to note that this older meaning seems to have been taken up nowadays by the so-called 'leftist' movements.

According to Ellul, revolt erupts only when a certain situation becomes established which offers no prospect of change. But yet again the social structures and the disparity between the social or political situation do not explain revolts satisfactorily. There can be economic causes (recession, want, etc.) or legal causes (such as an unequal distribution of taxes between social groups or between town and country), but one must not forget religious causes which are in no way, and this is contrary to Marxist beliefs, a reflection of socio-economic factors.

But ought one to consider this revolt–revolution distinction as absolute? Even those authors who are most sensitive to the distinction are not completely in favour of going this far. For Ellul, a revolution can grow out of a revolt and in this case it goes on to assume the characteristics of revolt. Yet before 1789, revolution comes about in the same way as revolt, that is, as a reaction against history. It is a denial of the future. To be otherwise, in addition to the insurgent 'masses', it would need the support of a theory and efficient organizers; now these were rare in the Middle Ages, and in later periods too. This may have been the case when there was some unity between a rural uprising and an urban movement (especially if the town was the capital of a kingdom or principality). Ellul does not mention the case of the 1358 Jacquerie which was linked with the Parisian burghers under the leadership of Etienne Marcel, because he doubtless believes – and rightly – that at no time was it a revolution. He quotes instead the English revolt of 1381 which indeed almost was revolutionary in character. The objectives of the peasants were both financial and social. But the people of London, the majority of whom joined with the country rebels, were pursuing aims which were mainly political: the burghers hardly shared the grievances of the country folk, preferring to criticize the actions of the Regent and the advisers of the young king. However, at first they all put on a united front and there was no 'class' struggle, since some nobles and clergy had already sided with the rebels. They demanded that the advisers, "traitors to the people and the king", be committed for trial, and claimed to remain loyal to the king, the revolt being in no way incompatible with this loyalty. The king was induced to make concessions and the Londoners then considered their victory as won; this led to the greater part of the peasant troops being demobilized. But, encouraged by these first political successes, Wat Tyler changed from being the leader of a revolt into the leader of a would-be revolution: his was a programme of complete social revolution which corresponded but little with the wishes of the rural masses: suppression of all 'sovereignty' other than that of the king, suppression of the bishops, distribution of the goods of the Church among the parishioners, etc., with only the emancipation of all serfs being of any consequence to the peasants. However, this leader turned revolutionary no longer had enough troops to try to launch the country into civil war. In any case, he was killed shortly after his personal 'metamorphosis'. Here then is a revolt which perhaps only just missed becoming a revolution: the backward-looking aspect of the revolt (the refusal to accept 'innovations' which nevertheless constituted definite progress in the way the state was governed) almost made way for a programme of complete social upheaval. But, even in these closing years to the fourteenth century which mark for some the birth of 'class' struggle (a concession which the Marxists would still judge to be quite inadequate since, for them, it was born much earlier), revolt led only to repression and not to revolution.

From all this, one will no doubt conclude that the examination of social change should be handled with greater prudence than modern-day sociology allows, for it has shown itself unable to penetrate satisfactorily the true nature of revolts. The fact remains, however, that the sociology of conflict, provided that one refines and adapts its assertions relating to the medieval and modern periods, can without question be very useful to the historian.

CHAPTER 3

The insurgents

Following our examination of the circumstances, conditions and general aspects of revolt or 'change', we must now turn our attention to the people involved. The main question that has to be asked is whether, at the root of a rebellion, there is one leader, one or several groups, or all these at the same time. If there is more than one 'leader', are the principal actors limited at first to a small group, or do they form almost immediately a group or several groups with many members? Are these groups, or the single group, homogeneous? We are thus faced with immense problems, but in studying them, we have been forced, through lack of space, to limit, for the moment, our number of concrete illustrations.

Social classes? Class conflict?

(A) The concept of social class

Mousnier has recently reminded us "that at the moment there is a flood of words and a mountain of paper resulting from the confusion of thoughts propagated amongst historians who do not give the same meaning to the same words". This statement is particularly apt with regard to the history of rebellion, which is so troubled by the concept of class; it is accepted without question by some medievalists who, in consequence, then go on to accept, rightly or wrongly, the Marxist idea of class conflict. Indeed, the existence of different classes and of an inevitable and general class conflict is too frequently considered as fact. Now a fact does not have to be proved, it is accepted. But is it really a question, in the circumstances, of facts? Then again, the term 'class' is too often used randomly with meanings which vary from one author to another.

According to Mousnier, "in the work of the historian, even though the concept of class can only be an abstraction, it presupposes an examination of man's totality, at one given time and in one given place, within the totality of the different social groups to which he belongs and within the totality of each one of these social groups". We must seek "man's totality within the social totality".

We can follow Mousnier in the consequences which he draws from these remarks. He feels unable to accept the opinions of those who think that "the totality is made up of a series of distinct and relatively autonomous levels: economic, political, religious, ideological, philosophical, artistic, scientific, but depending ultimately on the economic level which would be the dominant one". For them, in all forms of society one specified type of production and the profit it yields determines the rank and importance of 'profit' yielded by the other types of production, the aim of history being reduced to conceptualizing "the structure and method of a specified social formation, dependent on a clearly defined mode of production" (Louis Althusser). In this enumeration of levels, the social aspect disappears, so does man, and with man, all sense of reality.

Moreover, the concept of class embraces a hierarchy of concepts. There is no doubt that in Marx one is led through this whole series, from the enumeration of social classes to the definition of class itself.

(B) An examination of Marxist theses

If the word 'class' came before Karl Marx (compare, for example, its use by Henri de Saint-Simon), the concept was born in Marx's mind as the result of his analysis of the returns of capitalist production between 1838 and 1867 in England, particularly Manchester. Then, with dubious boldness, Marx made his rash generalizations, at the same time not losing sight of materialist principles, not to mention the old messianism.

One of the major ideas of Marxism is the notion of a proletariat, of a working class which is the agent of the historical process, the chosen one of history. But in order to arrive at this idea of a proletariat, did Marx institute an exhaustive study of the lower strata throughout the history of mankind?

Apart from the history through which he lived, Marx studied only one single historical period in depth – the French Revolution; it was an event of great significance, but, nevertheless, took place within relatively narrow confines. It was the bourgeoisie (as he, following others, called it) which provided him with the 'model' for the revolutionary class which rises in rebellion in order to gain some future profit; it was a model not only to be followed but to be excelled. For he had read the 'bourgeois' historians of the Restoration and the July Monarchy: Augustin Thierry, Guizot, Mignet, Thiers, Henri Martin and such. All these men were inspired with a sort of 'bourgeois messianism': they thought that the accession of the tax-paying bourgeoisie to the role of dominant managing groups was in some way the natural outcome of the whole of French history, which they conceived as a gradual rise of this bourgeoisie, a rise which had, since the Middle Ages, not been without its set-backs. From these historians, Marx took the idea of a *climbing* social category which, increasingly as it climbs, embodies both the general interests of society and the hope of a better future: it was the bourgeois of the medieval 'communes' who brought progress and hope for the future, and these 'communes' and their leaders – among them Etienne Marcel – were the precursors of the Revolution: before the era of Marxist historians, the 'bourgeois' historians saw only a difference of degree, not of kind, between medieval and modern rebellions on the one hand, and contemporary revolutions on the other.

But Marx is a Hegelian, and the victory of the bourgeoisie could not be either absolute nor terminal. The victory cannot be definitive, for this capitalist bourgeoisie, which possesses the means of production and exchange, subjects the majority of the population – a majority destined to become ever larger – to a growing exploitation: the peasants and other intermediate groups become proletarian in character. The proletariat swells in numbers and becomes more and more exploited by a bourgeoisie in which the wealth becomes more and more concentrated: Manchester is both the example and the prototype of what will soon be seen everywhere. And this proletariat is seen by Marx as the rising class which will replace the bourgeoisie (whose decline is inevitable) as a result of a revolutionary process. Basically, Hegel's philosophy, by which Marx, like many of his contemporaries, was greatly influenced, even if he did sometimes criticize it, was thought to justify this inevitable replacement of the bourgeoisie by the proletariat and the inevitable struggle between these two classes; and what is more, this philosophy was thought to offer better justification than historical examples, of which there were all too few.

The dialectical method was not created by Hegel. Reality as perceived by Heraclitus is a Becoming, a succession, because, through its movement in time, it stands in opposition to itself: "Becoming seems at conflict with itself; the opposing elements are sometimes discordant, and sometimes result in a harmony which ends all previous conflict, but which then meets a new opposing element." There are thus contrarieties rather than contradictions (a term which the Marxists use so readily). In Becoming, conflict plays a powerful role, and the elements in conflict are termed contrarieties precisely because they are in conflict, Being itself being a process. These are the essentials of the dialectic which, since the Greeks, has tempted many philosophers, even in the Middle Ages, as shown by the example of Nicholas of Cusa amongst others. But the neo-dialecticians of the nineteenth and twentieth centuries looked no further than Hegel for their inspiration.

For Hegel, the error committed before him was to make of antinomy, of contrariety, "a characteristic of the man who speaks and thinks, but not of the thing about which he speaks or thinks, not of the real itself". For him and those who follow him on this point (such as Marx, Engels and Lenin), "contradiction (Hegel substituted this word for *contrariety*) is the root of all movement and all life; it is in so far as it has a contradiction within itself that it moves, that it has impulsion and activity". *Negation*, that is, opposition, is the internal source of all spontaneous, living and spiritual movement. If the opposition is real, the inseparability of the opposites, their unity therefore, is also real, for existence is a unity which unites them. The relationship between the first and second term is one of negation. But there is necessarily a third which forms with them the Hegelian *triad* and which is the negation of negation: the major components of the preceding thesis and antithesis are at once exceeded by, and conserved in, the synthesis. Thus, within the flow of time, a Being remains itself only by becoming another thanks to its inner contradictions. Being and Not-being are in a state of permanent conflict, and it is Becoming which gives them unity. All this is assuredly a mode of thinking which belongs to a man acutely aware of history.

Can there be an end in this constantly renewed process of the Hegelian *triad*? No, in principle, since all synthesis changes immediately into thesis and since the cycle starts all over again, and is constantly renewed. Yet, Hegel already contradicts his own dialectic in foreseeing an end to this process, an end which will come about when the Spirit knows itself. But the Marxists have been much further in this direction by using dialectic (is not their doctrine *dialectical* materialism?) and by introducing it into their system. Now the dialectical method is inevitably in contradiction to every *system*, particularly a system which foresees as the end-result of history a classless society where, whatever the Marxists may sometimes say, the contradictions would all be transcended: there would be a stage of history, a final stage where the Hegelian triad would have become obsolete.

Hegel's philosophy owes much to an examination of the history of the end of the eighteenth and beginning of the nineteenth centuries; it is not even totally comprehensible without reference to the historical context. Already, the philosophy of Heraclitus owed much to the history of his time, a time of crises and fraught by social upheavals, thus a world at conflict with itself. As for Hegel, he attempted to present a composite *whole*, in his wish to express all that existed for him as true in the thinking of his period (according to him, the last of all periods) because his time "had denied but conserved (within itself) all preceding periods". Critical thought which had given such effective arms to the bourgeois in 1789 had opened the way for the destruction of everything which, perhaps, survived only through habit. But the 'conservative' thinking of a de Bonald or a Burke had recalled shortly afterwards that there is no law, religion or society except in a historical context because human nature is historical. In this passage from a thesis (revolutionary thought) to antithesis (counter-revolutionary and 'positive' thought), Hegel saw the very movement of his own time: to the 'natural' (that is to say, abstract) thinking of eighteenth-century *philosophers*, are opposed *positivity* and historicity; this is something that Auguste Comte was likewise to perceive.

From the Hegelian dialectic, the Marxists have kept in particular the idea that everything is relative. Thus, in Engels' opinion, one will "henceforth . . . be continually aware of the necessary relativity of all acquired knowledge, of its dependence with regard to the conditions in which it has been acquired". Nothing is fixed, a good can become an evil and vice versa, the true becomes false and what was necessary is so no more. Through Becoming, good will reveal the evil which it bears within it and the evil will disclose its good properties: the social consequences of these assertions (to say nothing of the moral consequences) are, of course, extremely important.

There is a way out of the contradictions which a society bears within itself; this solution is a new road which leads to a new state of society where the elements of the preceding terms will be both exceeded and conserved. Yet, for Marxism, this will not go on happening indefinitely and there will be a leap, a decisive change, as one passes from the relative to the absolute (which, yet again, is contrary to the dialectic itself). Monnerot has astutely commented that in Marxism, a non-evolutionary archetype can be seen in its prophecy that the classless society will bring an end to history in so far as "the history of mankind is simply the history of its class struggles", as *The Communist manifesto* proclaims. If the dialectic is right, the history of mankind is not simply the history of its class struggles. But the dialectic is not alone in suggesting this .... And Marxism can seem unfaithful to its own dialectical method by stressing economic primacy. For it contradicts the general dialectical interdependence to introduce the idea that some elements "would in short always be determinant, never determined", the economy never being anything except determinant of the social hierarchy, never being determined. It is true that one can discern some fluctuation in Marx on this point, perhaps because he had realized that his materialism was, in the last analysis, scarcely dialectical.

In the Marxist notion of society, there are relationships of forces – which in itself is undeniable. But, for Marx and Engels, a historical force is conquered and routed only when its positions give way beneath it, when a new historical force, in the construction of which the previous one has subconsciously worked, is powerful enough to supplant it. Through conflict, of course, not otherwise. Class conflict is indeed a dialectical necessity for Marxism, according to which there are always inner contradictions within a society; this will always be a class society until the return to primitive communism which will see the advent of the classless society. But the dialectic, modified by Marxism, is accompanied according to some, by a 'procession of mirages' which gives new life to the old myths. Engels wrote "We must not let ourselves be ruled ... by the irreducible antagonisms of the old metaphysics ..., antagonisms of the true and false, good and evil, the identical and the different". But these 'antagonisms' correspond to archetypes and as they are always inclined to reappear under different guises, might one not see them resurfacing in Marxism? Could one not see in the antagonism between classes, that between the bourgeoisie and the proletariat, a new form of the antagonism between Good and Evil, a rebirth of millenarianism?

Since, according to Marx and Engels, the classes are always in conflict, they had to examine the 'dialectical' basis of this conflict before being able to specify the Marxist notion of class, its value, its possible extension in time and space. How can one pass from an examination of the nineteenth-century bourgeoisie and the Manchester proletariat to a theory valid for all epochs, except the first and last? It is to be feared that the theory was arrived at by extrapolation from a few cases and because of a tendency to oversimplify, for the analyses were narrow and incomplete. Can it be said that just as the relationship between the infrastructure (the economy) and the superstructure is invariable, so the position of human groups in production and the status of ownership have always had the same fundamental importance?

Marx did not elaborate a complete theory of social classes since he died whilst working on his *Capital*. But one can draw together different passages from his work or refer, for example, to *The German ideology* which he wrote in collaboration with Engels. What forms a social class would be "at first sight the identity of the income with the source of the income". But as incomes differ in the same way that the forms of ownership differ, the classes are distinguished essentially by ownership or non-ownership of the means of production.

The degree of development of the productive forces is a function of the "development attained by the division of labour", and the "various stages of development in the division of labour are just so many different forms of ownership, that is, the existing stage in the division of labour determines also the relations of individuals to one another with reference to the material, instrument, and product of labour". We shall pass over the first two forms of ownership, that of the primitive 'tribe', then *communal* ownership (we mean by that the ownership of the ancient *polis*). The third is feudal ownership which medieval Christianity would have known: like all the other forms in their time, it alone was seen to be responsible for social differences, differences which Marxism condemns in the same way that it denies, in principle, all hierarchy in society.

The two authors confuse two different ideas when they write that "apart from the differentiation of princes, nobility, clergy and peasants in the country, and masters, journeymen, apprentices and soon also the rabble of casual labourers in the towns, no division [of labour] took place". Attention has been drawn to the significant words: 'differentiation' and 'division'. Without going to the other extreme, we recall that for a long time in certain trades, the master and his subordinates led more or less the same life. But, as a concluding comment on this idea of the weakness of the division of labour, let us note that, for Marx and Engels, the division of labour was rendered more difficult in agriculture "by the strip-system [yet there were, also, large units of cultivation] beside which the cottage industry of the peasants themselves emerged [an allusion, probably, to the domestic textile work carried on in certain rural regions near a weaving town]". Within the "industry, there was no division of labour at all in the individual trades themselves, and very little between them" which is less and less true especially from the thirteenth century onwards. As for the division between industry and commerce, although it existed in the "older towns", only later did it develop and grow in the newer towns, at a time "when the towns entered into mutual relations": if the suggestion is that there was commercial precapitalism in the textile industry, then this is probably right.

Finally, "the grouping of larger territories into feudal kingdoms was a necessity for the landed nobility [this is very debatable and there is no lack of examples to the contrary] and for the towns"; the Flemish towns, however, held different views .... For Marx and Engels, "the organization of the ruling class, the nobility, had everywhere a monarch at its head". For them, the king could only be the agent of the nobles whom he was helping to extort surplus-labour from the exploited. The governors would thus be characterized by a "specific difference in relation to the governed" (Monnerot) because all those governed would be exploited. Consequently, a revolt against the nobility would also be a revolt against the king. But medieval and modern history is far from confirming this.

For a composite view of the origins of the bourgeoisie, it is better to refer also to the *The Communist manifesto* which completes the explanations given in *The German ideology*. "From the serfs of the Middle Ages sprang the chartered burghers of the earliest towns. From these burgesses the first elements of the bourgeoisie were developed." These first bourgeois were "compelled to unite against the landed nobility to save their skins", a statement which renders a very incomplete account of the 'communal' revolts themselves. It was only very slowly that the bourgeoisie as a class was formed from numerous local bourgeois groups in different towns. And "the burghers had created the conditions [of life] in so far as they had torn themselves free from feudal ties". These conditions common to all and determined by bourgeois opposition "to the feudal system which they found in existence", developed into class conditions once the 'link' had been effected between the towns. This happened because "separate individuals form a class only in so far as they have to carry on a common battle against another class", in this case the nobility, the ruling class. So the bourgeoisie was going to begin to play in history "a most revolutionary part" for "all revolutionary struggle is directed against a class which has hitherto dominated". Thus it was on "the ruins of feudal society" that the bourgeoisie was going to rest its power. But in its turn, it was going to create "new conditions of oppression" apparently even before the end of the Middle Ages, subjecting, for example, the country to the rule of the towns, although this is scarcely proven except for the end of the medieval period and principally with regard to Italy. As for the king and the state, they were going to become the executive of the bourgeoisie.

We shall not dwell on the vagueness of the chronology which must embarrass any historian on reading these categorical texts; neither shall we dwell on the dialectical aspect of class oppositions nor the fact that, in this way of looking at things, the birth and development of the bourgeoisie were made possible only through its opposition to the class which up to then had been dominant in feudalism, the nobility. There are many medieval examples of the frequent harmony between nobles and bourgeois. In the same way, the peasant–nobility opposition was not endemically rife. And to say that the state is the figure-head and engine of war of the ruling class, the nobility, is, on the whole, a groundless assertion. The French monarchy depended on the bourgeoisie fairly early on, if not from Louis VI's reign as was claimed until recently, at least from Philip II's, although this did not necessarily involve its entering into open conflict with the nobility. After being the so-called agent of the nobles, it thus did not become the agent of the bourgeoisie. And in England it was often a coalition of the nobles and "communes" which made life difficult for the Plantagenets during the thirteenth century. In short, popular revolts may have been nourished by other social groups in whom, however, Marxism sees only 'exploiters' of the people.

Can one really formulate a theory wherein the notion of surplus-labour is the basis of the class concept? We can join Mousnier in being sceptical. Yet it is what Marx wrote in *Capital*: "Wherever a part of society possesses the monopoly of the means of production, the labourer, free or not free, must add to the working time necessary for his own maintenance an extra working time in order to produce the means of subsistence for the owners of the means of production." And Marx gives profuse examples taken from divers societies: his exploiters are Athenian nobles, Etruscan theocrats, Wallachian boyars, medieval lords and modern capitalists. "Does it really make sense to give them all the same label?", asks Mousnier, "Is the so-called fundamental relationship, which allows the unifying of such diversity, really fundamental to every case?" It is certainly hazardous to build a general social theory on the notion of surplus-labour. Even if it is true that the division of labour was still undeveloped in the Middle Ages, it existed and made distinct progress from the eleventh century onwards. Now, "as soon as there is a division of labour, everyone is obliged to produce surplus-labour in order to pay for the service of others, everyone and not just the manufacturers of material goods, but intellectuals as well as manual workers, administrators as well as the administered and soldiers as well as civilians. To want to consider only manual surplus-labour, producing material goods, is to falsify everything. What we must look at is the totality of social labour" concludes Mousnier. And it is obvious that, for example in the Middle Ages, the peasants and the bourgeois needed a protection which only the aristocracy and then the nobility could provide. Revolts broke out precisely when the French nobility, during the first phase of the Hundred Years War, was judged incapable of protecting its people.

The social strata

Although it does not have the characteristics which Marx believed were universally applicable to it, the hierarchical structure of social groups is an undeniable fact. But the class society – which does not, however, inevitably imply class conflict – appears only in a market economy "where the highest social value is placed on the production of material goods, where the highest esteem, honour and social dignity go to the undertaker of such a production, where it is the role played in the method of production of material goods and (to a lesser degree) the money earned by this role which place individuals on the different rungs of the social hierarchy". In the nineteenth century, and only in that century, typical class societies existed in Western Europe and North America; nowhere else and no earlier. All that one does find before this are rare prefigurements of a class society, for example, in some towns from the end of the Middle Ages onwards.

Since the word 'class' has had too specific a meaning since Marx, and since it does not correspond to reality either in the Middle Ages or the more modern period, we must choose another word to indicate a truly universal concept, a concept which will thus be applicable to the whole of the Middle Ages. And if one turns to Mousnier, one will find that he has made wide use of the term *strata* for the modern period, and medievalists would be well advised to adopt this term.

(A) The general perspective

There is always social stratification. Ever since the time of the ancient Greeks, philosophers such as Plato have described the society of their time as being composed of human groups forming kinds of social layers, thus strata, superimposed on one another in a sort of hierarchy. But this stratification does not result only from social *differentiation*, it also comes from social *evaluation*. The first has, as its origin, the division of social labour, the second comes from the fact that "social functions are evaluated differently according to the established circumstances in which the societies live".

A social stratum is at first characterized in relation to the division of labour. What part of the social labour is given to its members, for example in the military, spiritual and manufacturing spheres? A stratum is also characterized by the form of this social labour and the degree to which it disposes of the social labour of one or several other strata. "In the beginning was co-operation" (Mousnier) and the division of social labour is clear proof of this. But this proof in no way implies an idyllic vision of life and social relationships; on the contrary, it has to do with the sociology of conflict. It is from here that the will for power comes: "With the birth of the social strata, there comes a rivalry between strata and, if the relationships of co-operation are fundamental, there springs from this rivalry quite a different side to social relationships–antagonistic relationships."

The evaluation of social functions lies in value judgements, often implicit, on "the necessity, utility, importance, dignity, honour and grandeur of the different social functions". These value judgements differ according to the societies, which comes back to saying that "systems of social stratification are all different from one another, although they may be reduced to set-types". These judgements are based on the power, real or imaginary, which the society in question attributes to any one function; they come "not from precise ideas and facts, but from beliefs, impressions and opinions which are most frequently suggested by the emotions or sentimental and affective inclinations and which are perfectly irrational and largely erroneous". Yet, the opinions at the root of the evaluation of social functions always contain a certain amount of truth. If religion is judged to be more important than all the other functions, the religious function of the priest will be at the top of the social hierarchy. If war and unrest are endemic, military functions will be at the top. But if it is material life and the satisfaction of physical needs and pleasure which are placed above everything, the production of economic goods will be judged essential.

Is it true, as Marx and Engels thought, that the division of social labour carries with it the alienation of man and ties him down to one exclusive activity from which only communism can free him? In fact, the theory of alienation from which the men of the Middle Ages, like those of other times, supposedly suffered, can seem specious: such a theory would find it very difficult to account for revolts and even revolutions. If we are to believe *The German ideology*, in a communist society alienation would disappear and society itself would regulate the general production, allowing the same man a diversity of activities: he could be in turn a labourer, civil servant, intellectual, etc. Yet social progress is linked to the growth of the division of labour: even Marx and Engels seemed to subscribe to this commonsense observation in their critique of feudalism, only to lose sight of it soon after. As Mousnier states, "to give the same man a diversity of occupations will only make of him a jack of all trades".

Social class is only a genus, a general concept within the universal concept of the family of social strata. Neither the Middle Ages nor the following period knew this genus, which did not assert itself until the nineteenth century. They knew another genus, another general concept, that of *Order*.

(B) Societies composed of Orders

A society of Orders is based on "the social esteem, dignity and honour accorded by general agreement to some social function which may have no direct connection with the production of material goods. The fundamental principle of organization of these societies has its base in each of these agreements". The number of types of societies of Orders corresponds to the number of principles.

The Middle Ages did not consider that everything which concerned material goods was of supreme importance. To speak of classes in the Marxist sense is completely to misunderstand medieval history. For it is impossible to understand the eleven or so centuries of this most important period in the history of mankind if one ignores the place – the supremely important place – occupied by religion, especially from the Carolingian period onwards and right through to the end of the Middle Ages even (how, if we ignore it, are we to understand the two Reformations, one Protestant, one Catholic, which came about in the sixteenth century?).

Those who govern are not by definition exploiters, their first duty being to rule the earthly City in such a way that men can prepare themselves for the City of God. The great philosophers and theologians of the twelfth and thirteenth centuries said nothing new, even if they said it better than their predecessors: society is neither materialistic nor productivist. Thus, producers in the economic sense, peasants, craftsmen and merchants too, are not considered as determinant elements in Christian society. Producers exist because they are necessary, not, in fact, because they are 'good': the Platonic distinction between the Necessary and the Good has been taken up again by Christianity. Mankind would obviously die if there were no producers but the ultimate objective of mankind is not to exist on earth and it cannot therefore justify its existence in terms of itself. It has been said: "For medieval man, Earth, which he does not leave during his lifetime and which nourishes him, gives him no command, it is to the heavens that he raises his eyes; man is distinguished not by what *conditions* him, but by that to which he aspires." This recalls St Paul's *Conversatio nostra in coelis est.* Martial power, the necessity for which cannot be doubted in view of the internal and external conditions of medieval society, more or less claimed to exist as a good, but the quarrel over lay investiture between the Empire and papacy and many other conflicts between temporal and spiritual power, show that this claim has always been a matter of dispute. Finally, and logically, in such a society it is the clergy who must be placed at the top of the social hierarchy. Material goods must be provided by the producers for those who pray and lead the *populus Christianus* towards God and for the warriors (the aristocracy then the nobility) who must defend the people against pagans and all possible dangers created by man; the goods must be provided in exchange for these indispensable services. Collaboration between all the social strata is indispensable; Christianity is a body politic whose unity is completely unshakeable since all its people, all its strata, have a common denominator, namely, membership of the Church.

If the lower order thus supports the higher, it is not to say that it controls it in any way, for this was not what God intended when He placed the lower order in its 'estate'. Indeed, the fate of the lowly was often difficult, especially during the early Middle Ages and also (and fairly often) in the fourteenth and fifteenth centuries, even though Marx, as has been pointed out, blackened the picture in reaction to Saint-Simon and especially Auguste Comte who were too inclined, for their part, to see only the bright side of things. But Saint-Simon and Comte went no further than St Thomas Aquinas and his contemporaries who, like their predecessors in the early Middle Ages, never dreamed that the lower strata were, or should be, in a "state of psychological and moral secession in relation to the rest of society". For this, in short, is the Marxist assumption which is widespread in contemporary thought and according to which the lower strata, because they are at the bottom of the hierarchy, do not accept the social order such as it is despite deceptive appearances to the contrary: revolt, although latent, is always present and is only waiting for an opportunity to erupt. But no one has ever succeeded in demonstrating the correctness of this assumption for the medieval period. A non-communist form of society where everybody would accept his place seemed totally inconceivable to Marx, or rather, immoral, because religion – and this is the major reproach made to the 'opium of the people' – works scandalously to make the lower strata accept their position. But should one revolt because one has been placed in a lower stratum? Or only because one thinks one has been placed there unjustly? To the great thinkers of the Middle Ages a negative answer to both these questions seemed the only one possible.

In European society, and up to the eighteenth century, society was thought of as 'established society'. Dating from long before Christianity, since we find it, for example, in the Greek cities, the idea of 'established society' was clearly set out by Christian thinkers, nobody as yet having shown that they were in contradiction – flagrant contradiction – with the social mentality of their time. So we can refer to St Thomas Aquinas precisely because he put forward a *summa* of all Christian thought. The social order is permeated with the divine, each of its elements has its place there, as desired by God, and all beings are necessary to this Order. For all men are part of the economy of Providence: they all have the same worth, even though they are not equal and they are each and every one irreplaceable because they are all necessary from God's point of view. Consequently, no social function is useless and none should be scorned. As the human condition is transient, each human being must come to terms as best he can with the ordeal of life's journey, not forgetting that his earthly life is only a limited role.

For the theologians society is indeed hierarchical. So one must submit to the political order if it conforms with religion – a significant restriction – for all power comes from God. And one can be Christian whether one is a lord or serf, a fact which the Fathers of the Church had already proclaimed. Consequently, revolt is inadmissible, apart from rare and very specific exceptions. One ought not to try to escape one's mortal condition but resolve, as best one can, the problem of one's personal salvation as well as that of the 'common good'.

The Thomist notion, which brought nothing very new to the thirteenth century, perhaps idealized reality. It certainly did when Thomism laid down what *ought* to be. But nobody has shown – except by a naive use of Marxist terms – that the refusal of the Order by the lower strata was "a fact fundamental to, and immanent in, history" (Monnerot) nor that it was widespread in the Middle Ages outside millenarian circles. But Thomism reveals, or confirms, a fairly general attitude of mind. For the Church, poverty is not necessarily good, nor wealth and power necessarily bad. In a society steeped in faith, the poor man fears Hell, but the powerful or rich fear it much more. There are thus unseen restraints because both the powerful and the weak judge themselves in the eyes of one God. But that in no way excludes the possibility of violent unrest nor, of course, the persistence of eschatological myths. The simple truth is that unrest and myth only rarely called into question the Christian Order as a whole; the insurgent groups that went this far were small and unrepresentative of any stratum. Fear of the devil played a considerable social role in the Middle Ages.

The Christian 'Order' led to a society of 'Orders': it is not by chance that the same word has these two meanings. Although the Orders were not to combine their *de facto* existence with an incipient *de jure* existence until the end of the Middle Ages, they had, in fact, taken shape much earlier.

The Orders appeared in theoretical form in the Carolingian era. At that time Charlemagne's Church leaders took up an idea of Valentinus: everyone has his place, there is social harmony, God has placed each man in a 'group' (another meaning of the term *ordo*) and given him a function (*ministerium*) to carry out. In Louis the Pious' *Notice to the Orders of the kingdom* we read that the sovereign himself occupies a place designated by God, and it is his duty to be the guide and moral head of his subjects. Historians have deduced, perhaps a little hastily, that this was a condemnation of all change, thus an indication of clearly defined conservatism. This is by no means certain, however, since the word 'change' can have several meanings and one could well argue that the condemnation was directed at disorderly change or change associated with violence.

For Bishop Theodulf of Orleans, society is divided into three *ordines*: the monks who live at the foot of the throne of God, the clergy who prepare the faithful for salvation, and the laity who "turn the wheel of the mill". This was both unduly favourable to the men of the Church and did not distinguish the warriors from the producers. Hence the considerable modifications which the theory subsequently had to undergo. In any case, the major judicial distinction in Frankish law, that contrasting freemen and serfs, could never have a place in any theory of Orders. Neither, it stands to reason despite certain appearances, could pure economic criteria. It is true that, as early as the middle of the eighth century, St Boniface, basing his theories on those of St Paul, had asserted that there is an *Order* of leaders, an *Order* of subjects, an *Order* of the rich and an *Order* of the powerful, each one obliged to follow the path traced for it by God. This differentiation of four *Orders*, a differentiation which did not survive, had moral and not economic overtones. A 'new awareness' has been spoken of in connection with certain theoreticians, particularly Jonas of Orleans because he preached against the rich and the *potentes* who should know that "in their essential nature, their serfs and all the poor are their equals". But one cannot mix the moral and religious, and this is what is at issue here (note the word 'nature'), with the economic. All those – and there are many – who, through the centuries, spoke or wrote in favour of the poor, were not, by this very fact, condemning the entire economic system, neither did they desire a complete transformation of society: it was only the wicked rich, as in the gospels, who were condemned by the clergy. There is nothing here which suggests a condemnation of the whole social system. An awareness of the tares in a society is not necessarily, as a widespread Marxist notion has convinced many of our contemporaries, an awareness of the exploitation of one whole group by another nor, especially, is it an awareness of the necessity of rousing any dormant class conflict.

The mutual services which the Orders must render one another allow the supremacy of the Christian Order. This is what the theoreticians never cease proclaiming. But the outlook of the Carolingian *ordines* was much modified in the course of time because of its wish to stick closer to reality. This shows that the tendency to immobility with which one credits the men of the Church ("the social world is unchangeable, only thus does it conform with divine law") has to be viewed with a degree of critical subtlety. For it was the clergy – practically only they were capable of writing – who elaborated the new typologies of the Orders, of which one is directly inspired by social reality: as opposed to the single body of the clergy, whose pre-eminence cannot be disputed in a predominantly religious society, one finds a laity in which it is necessary to distinguish more than one level. At least two, in fact: there are the men who fight (we are speaking of a society which is also predominantly martial) and those who produce material goods. Thus one can distinguish the *oratores* (those who pray, therefore all the clergy), the *bellatores* (those who wage war) and the *agricultores* (the country folk). So thought Ratheri of Verona (died 974) and Adalbero of Laon (died 1030). In his *Poem to King Robert* (the Pious), Adalbero expressed a generally held view which was to last for centuries: "The City of God which is thought to be one entity, is divided into three: some pray, others fight and others work [the word is *laboratores*, whose meaning is wider, in principle, than that of *agricultores*]. These three Orders which coexist would not bear separation. The services rendered by the one allow the work of the other two. Each in turn undertakes to lighten the burden of the whole." On the other hand, it is true that Adalbero does distinguish within this society (a single entity in the eyes of Providence) two separate *estates*, that of the free and that of the serfs. This is understandable because at the beginning of the eleventh century, serfdom was widespread but, with its almost general decrease, this differentiation of two estates, inherited moreover from the Fathers of the Church, was subsequently abandoned. But it was not Adalbero's intention that this distinction should challenge the traditional distinction between the three Orders. In any case, if authors have justifiably noted that he complains of the collapse of the ideal inherent in the typology of the three Orders, one must not conclude therefrom that this typology was useless. A society obviously never coincides with an ideal: it only more or less approaches it or recedes from it according to moment and circumstance.

Can one seriously propose that the concept of a hierarchical Order, made up of *ordines* and handed down from St Paul and St Augustine by way of the Carolingians, was nothing more than the achievement of backward-looking minds or of men completely out of touch with social reality? The concept would not have survived so long and it would not have evolved ultimately into orders playing a role as such and recognized by the state, as was the case up to 1789 (and not only in France). Moreover, this whole theory of Orders was evolutionary precisely because it corresponded to a deep-seated tendency in the collective mentality. After St Bernard who, even in the middle of the twelfth century, still insisted on the complementary relationship between the three Orders and the obligation of every man to submit to the vocation (*obedientia*) of his particular Order, the theory was substantially, although not fundamentally, modified to make it more compatible with the social evolution which had mainly come about through the rise of the towns and the growing number of bourgeois, merchants and artisans. Indeed, Ratheri of Verona had distinguished the merchants from the peasants much earlier (before the end of the tenth century, before the new urban growth of the eleventh to the thirteenth centuries); and Adalbero, as we have seen, substituted the term *laboratores* for *agricultores* (but for a long time the man who tilled the land was deemed the worker *par excellence*).

As early as the second half of the twelfth century, men such as Etienne of Fougères put forward, alongside the notion of Order, that of *estate* (*status*), but it no longer had Adalbero's meaning. This term, as we well know, enjoyed a long-lasting success. Following the growth of urban trades and the division of labour, there occurred a fragmentation of the third Order, that of the *laboratores*, a word brought permanently into fashion by St Bernard. But it would be incorrect to speak, as has been done, of substituting the notion of *estate* for that of *Order*: the two were in truth complementary and the second remained necessary as long as one believed that the union of all Christians was a reality. But it is true that one was sometimes taken for the other, and the Third Estate was in fact the third Order of the Kingdom of France.

Whether one looks to John of Salisbury, John of Freiburg or Innocent III, one finds total agreement: all the groups, which are not distinguished from each other by economic criteria but according to the part they play in the social labour, must be interdependent; and they are inseparable. The clergy are the heart, the princes the head, the nobles the arm holding the sword, and the burghers, merchants, artisans and peasants are the limbs or abdomen. And the term *conditio* which indicates the role of each man cannot be used, in its correct definition, to denote opposition between the different possible conditions, nor to imply necessarily and above all economic overtones. Moreover, the West in medieval times, we remember, was not alone in the history of mankind in its determination to stress the importance of the indispensable solidarity which should unite all humanity. There are many examples in Antiquity. The West simply maintained that, if society forms an organic whole and is based on association, it is because it is governed by a common recognition of normative values, namely the Christian values. Very close to our own time, this assertion is to be found, for example, in the writings of the Russian philosopher, Nicolas Berdyaev, where it springs from a reaction against the 'socialist' society and the idea of class conflict: although Berdyaev left the USSR as long ago as 1922, there is today, in certain Eastern European countries, a significant resurgence in the influence exerted by the works of this orthodox thinker.

In talking of solidarity between the Orders, some historians have readily set apart the fourteenth and fifteenth centuries because they witnessed more revolts than the preceding period (or perhaps simply these revolts are better known). In their eyes, union and solidarity between the Orders during this period is mere illusion, even more illusory than during earlier periods. As an argument against this view one could first of all invoke the persistence of writings on the idea of a society which was providential because willed by God. Under St Louis, Beaumanoir had taken up this idea and he had imitators at the end of the Middle Ages, despite the harshness of the times for many unfortunates. During the reign of Charles V, NICOLAS Oresme, although sensitive to the growing role of money in social relations, again invoked the indispensable nature of solidarity between the social strata or the Orders. And in 1420, when civil and foreign wars were devastating the kingdom, Alain Chartier, in his admirable *Quadrilogue invectif*, made no attempt to preach class conflict: it is wrong to see in his work a criticism of the surplus-value and surplus-labour which are denied the peasant or the artisan. The people, the nobles and the clergy all blame each other, and France, for her part, blames all three: it is not a complaint of the exploited (peasants and artisans) against the exploiters (clergy and nobles), since each group claims that the other is doing the exploiting. It is by no means certain that the social thinking of the end of the Middle Ages should be considered as impoverished in contrast to the richness and power of the philosophical thinking in an age which was precisely that in which the princes, if not the towns, launched themselves along the path of premercantilism, which necessarily carries with it social 'overlapping'. It was on the urban level that the notion of common good declined. Even if material preoccupations grew on the level of the state, economic factors were not yet placed above everything in the courts of France.

And it was in the fourteenth and fifteenth centuries, moreover, that decisive progress was made in the stratification of society into Orders, a stratification which was more than a mere herald of the society of Orders of early modern Europe. Phillippe de Vitry, a secretary to Philip VI of Valois, was not just returning to the old but sound concept of trinitarian society – trinitarian, too, because in God's image – when he wrote in 1335: "The People, in order better to evade the evils which it sees upon it, thus formed itself into three parts. One was formed to pray to God, the second to trade and work the land, and then, to keep these two groups from harm and injury, knights were created." Here, the word 'people' means all the subjects of the kingdom and the trinitarian organization is presented as being a *considered* decision of the people. The theory was now ready to take its place in the institutions of the realm. We now know for certain that the first estates, whether 'general' or not, go back only to the middle of the fourteenth century. But prior to that, the French monarchy had already begun making use of the division of its subjects into three Orders, the *de facto* existence of which was recognized by the sovereigns. One of the first consultations of public opinion in France goes back to the time of the struggle between Philip the Fair and Boniface VIII: now although the Louvre assembly, called by the king on 12 March 1303, was composed for the most part of prelates and high nobles, there might already have been some delegates present from large towns. Later on, before the outbreak of the Hundred Years War, there were no true States General. Yet, on several occasions, the kings convoked assemblies bringing together the representatives of the three Orders, thus officially recognizing their existence. Then, in 1347, estates were convoked within the framework of the *bailliages*: in the provostship and viscountcy of Paris (the Paris *bailliage*) men of the Church, nobles and non-nobles sat together. Finally, the first States General – those of 1355–1357 – included delegates from the three Orders. Taking advantage of the disasters of the war and all sorts of other difficulties (the imprisonment of John the Good in 1356, for example), it was the elected members from the towns and some royal officers who made the laws, the clergy and nobles (the latter having been brought into disrepute by their military set-backs) being brow-beaten and paralysed.

The stratification into Orders was no longer merely realized as a fact, it had just been recognized in public law. The society of Orders moves out of its prehistory into its history. But as Mousnier has shown, it was a military society of orders and continued to be so up until the eighteenth century. It is true that in law the ecclesiastical Order occupied first place since God's ministers had to keep "the highest rung of honour" (as Loyseau was to write in 1610); the Order of the nobility was given only second place. But in the early modern period, as in the Middle Ages, the Order of the nobility was the most important socially "and the one towards which everyone aimed" (Mousnier). Officers, burghers and merchants did not wait for the end of the medieval period to usurp, or at least try to usurp, the rank of noble: prestige, honorary (and fiscal . . .) privileges explain this long-lasting tendency in French society. At first, in the most troubled centuries of the Middle Ages, it was understandable that the aristocrats and then the nobility should have imposed their mark on the whole of society, especially since many prelates were recruited from their ranks. But, even in calm periods, or when the monarchy became strong enough itself to make public order respected, the stratification remained predominantly military because the nobles remained the warriors *par excellence.*

For the feudal era (we use the word 'feudal' in its true sense), Marc Bloch talked of the "noble class". The expression has since been taken up several times and it is claimed that the nobility constituted a social class rather than an Order because the stratification into Orders had only *de jure* validity. And, according to this view, the nobility was a social class before being a 'legal' class, something which did not come about until it wished to close ranks and, for that reason, form a clearly defined Order. But once the ranks were closed (and this does not correspond with the true facts), it would remain a social class because of its way of life – an expression wrongly restricted to the economic plane only: this way of life consisted in spending, and wasting, the "surplus-product accumulated by the peasants". In other words, the way of life, from its material aspect alone, would be the criterion of nobility. But even from this point of view, there were, in the Middle Ages and later, several noble 'ways of life': an immense gulf separated those lords who were richly possessed of fine properties from those whom we have called the *plèbe nobiliaire* and who had no more landed property than the poorest peasants.

What made the unity – but not the homogeneity – of the nobility, was not primarily the possession of important lordships which allowed a life of idleness without any need to bother with their administration (in reality, it is no longer commonly thought that the rural lords, from about the thirteenth century on, lived off their income from the land). It was rather the military way of life and the prestige and privileges which gradually came to be associated with it. The impoverished nobles were more respected than the rich merchants and the proof is that the latter, not only in France, took a pride in copying the nobility and in trying to infiltrate its ranks: the prestige of knighthood was great in the third Order: we may note the case of the young St Francis of Assisi, the son of a merchant, or that of the Florentine *popolani* who dubbed themselves knights in 1378.

The prestige of the second Order, its *de facto* pre-eminence, was not essentially due to money. What counted most was that the noble could boast the title of lord; even if, as far as land was concerned, his seigneury was no larger than certain rural tenements, he was none the less the owner of a seigneury, levying at least a few shillings rent from the peasants, his tenant-farmers, and exercising laws, however insignificant they might be; and, of course, there were the purely honorary privileges such as the right to have a coat of arms. A merchant might force a noble, his debtor, to sell him a fief in order to pay off his debt – something which was seen fairly often, particularly from the thirteenth century – but possession of this fief did not ennoble him and he even owed the king the frank-fee dues: he remained subject to the taxes of the 'common people', to tallage, for example. It was a slow process for such a burgher to gain acceptance as a noble; indeed, it would not be he but his son or grandson who finally gained acceptance, and this provided that life was lived in a noble manner, that there was no involvement in business (this was the case in France), and that a military calling was followed. For the wearing of the sword carried an unquestionable prestige at the end of the Middle Ages (this was still partly the case up until the beginning of the industrial era). The noble remained the supreme warrior who served the king in the 'noble' arm of the military profession, the cavalry. Indeed, the misfortunes of the nobility during the Hundred Years War were partly due to the fact that it could not gain a victory, nor even, at Poitiers, prevent the king from being taken prisoner. Even at a time when some nobles were nothing but pilferers (up to the twelfth century in France), the idea was very firmly entrenched in public opinion that the noble prerogatives were justified because the second Order was that of the sword and the defender of the realm.

The third Order – which was called the third estate until 1789 – had many more members and was of a much more mixed composition. It had more subdivisions – 'ranks', 'degrees', as they were to be called from the sixteenth century onwards – than each of the other two Orders. On the level of merchants and farm workers, especially the former, and because precapitalism, at first commercial, was born well before 1500, there very timidly took shape a class society which was to interfere one day with the society of statutes. But the process was so slow that only its faint outlines could be glimpsed at the end of the Middle Ages, and then almost solely in the largest and economically most active towns.

(C) Were the Orders the agents of rebellion?

For the seventeenth century, Mousnier has noted that there was conflict among the Orders, particularly between the magistrature and the *gentilshommes* (it was this conflict which caused the monarchy its celebrated difficulties). But in the fourteenth and fifteenth centuries, conflict between the legal profession and the men of the sword or between the nobility and powerful commoners was not yet fashionable. In other words, the conflict of Orders was not a medieval phenomenon.

Before 1500, there were no absolute dividing-lines between the three Orders. We know, obviously, who belonged to the first Order: one had to be a cleric, but there were clerics from noble, bourgeois, artisan and peasant origins. We also know, in principle, who was noble and who was not. But in fact, a difficulty (with which the men of the end of the Middle Ages came to terms) arose with the growth of the royal power and its 'bureaucracy' which initiated the creation of more and more offices. For neither the second nor the third Order ever had a monopoly amongst the royal officials, even high-ranking ones: nobles and burghers found themselves side by side in the highest posts. Both among the commoners and the nobles a distinction must be made between those who were officers – and great prestige went with the exercising of some of the royal or princely power – and those who were not. There was an office-holding bourgeoisie and an office-holding nobility, as opposed to a merchant or artisan bourgeoisie and a nobility which continued to engage in the military profession only. Was a nobleman who held office closer to a nobleman who did not than to a commoner who held office?

Neither the nobility nor the bourgeoisie was a homogeneous group, and this was so well before the appearance of administrative offices. Since the eleventh or twelfth centuries the burghers had not formed one united whole: the patriciate and the commonalty had quickly marked themselves off from each other, and often bitterly and violently opposed one another. And amongst the first bourgeois, then amongst those who came later into the bourgeoisie, there had been noblemen's sons, just as, at different periods, there had been burghers' sons amongst the nobility. The bourgeoisie, as one knows, was not born and did not develop to counteract 'feudalism' as seen by Marxism. If Western history is indeed characterized by the almost continuous rise of the bourgeoisie, it is not characterized correlatively by the continuous decline of the nobility; the decline which started around 1200 waited more than 500 years before it was complete. The nobility, as L. Genicot has shown, gained new strength on several occasions. On the one hand, each new dynasty created for itself its own nobility but without destroying the old one: this is what the first Valois did in the fourteenth century. Then again, at all times (not just in Madame de Sévigné's day), marriages between noble houses and bourgeois families were frequent, notably, but not solely, to rescue the lands of impoverished lords.

The creation of numerous offices in the last centuries of the Middle Ages provided a new bridge between nobility and bourgeoisie. For it was then that a powerful group was formed which lived from its service to the king (or prince, for example, in the Burgundian state) and which lived for him: it was not a class, since the officers did not fulfil an economic function. Until there is agreement on a better term, we shall use that of 'notables' (which is commonplace in the Middle Ages) to designate its members. Notables of the commonalty and notables of noble ancestry were firmly united with a very strong feeling of belonging to the same group, as is unquestionably shown by the history of the province wherein lay the seat of the French king. In the Ile-de-France of the closing years of the Middle Ages, there is clear evidence of intermixture between noble families, rich in rural lordships, and common lineages, owning little in the country, both of whom earned their living from royal offices. From the 1300s, when the state reasserted its power, from the time when the great bodies of the state (as they were to be called later) were given a more precise and judicious formulation, the group involved in the running of the principal institutions (especially the *Parlement*, the *Chambre des comptes*, etc.) was made up of noblemen or the sons of knights, and important bourgeois or descendants of powerful bourgeois families. Certain of these latter, moreover, were sooner or later to be ennobled either by sovereign decree or because, from the second half of the fifteenth century, the highest offices carried with them 'virtual nobility', that is, a promise of nobility, or because they simply made the usurping of nobility easier. For the crown was not reluctant to ennoble its burghers, at least those burghers who held offices; it was much less liberal with the merchant burghers, except under Louis XI.

Marc Bloch had rightly perceived that even before being ennobled in this way by the king (in future the only way, in France, one could be raised from the commonalty), some powerful burghers were already *de facto* aristocrats: amongst the most prominent families in history were the d'Orgemonts, lords of Chantilly among other places (thus, exceptionally, already well provided for in the country), the Braques, Budés, the Jouvenal des Ursins and the Briçonnets. It must have been the same, at least to some extent, for certain notables of lower rank, for example the magistrates of secondary jurisdictions such as the *Châtelet* of Paris (= tribunal of the provostship and viscountcy), who ended up, although later than the others, by creating important lordships for themselves, such as the Piedefer lineage. Now one sees all these notables, including those who were not entirely deserving of the title (the secondary ranking officers), follow the same policy; they forged numerous unions between families, thus taking, as it were, 'short cuts'. And the case of those *Parlement* members of humble extraction is but one illustration of the essential difference between social strata and classes: these commoners, who for a long time had few possessions in the country and who were poorer than many Parisian merchants, were, nevertheless, more highly respected than them; they were placed higher in the social hierarchy, almost on a level with the legal nobility.

The only conflict discernable in the fourteenth century is precisely that between the world of offices and that of trade. There were, certainly, officials who supported Etienne Marcel, the merchants' provost, but they were only a minority. On the whole, the merchants envied the office-holding commoners (just as they envied the office-holding noblemen), but after the Parisian pseudo-revolution of 1358, their jealousy subsided and changed into a desire to obtain office. A bridge was even constructed between certain business burghers, the financiers, and the office-holding burghers. In Paris, the money-changers and bankers, of merchant stock, tended to leave their profession more and more to enter the king's service, more particularly financial institutions, in the first instance the *Chambre des comptes*. It was in this way that in the fifteenth century part of the business bourgeoisie, and not the poorest, entered the world of the office-holding notables: a new stratum thus came to enlarge a world which still, nevertheless, did not constitute a social class, since the prestige attached to serving the king was more sought after than the wages which were, after all, fairly modest – in spite of various perquisites – and since greatly differing fortunes were to be found side by side amongst these notables.

One social sector thus remained vaguely situated in respect to the second and third Orders: it belonged to both. But this was only a temporary situation, since in the early modern period all the magistrates and administrators were placed in the third estate, despite their protests, which were, moreover, sometimes effective. This vagueness was not just because of the fact that the legal delimitation of the Orders was not yet complete at the end of the Middle Ages. It was also because of a phenomenon which R. Cazelles noted a few years ago, namely that at the beginning of the fourteenth century there arose a strong feeling which would have led to the removal of the distinction between nobles and non-nobles for the benefit of a new aristocracy, that of the king's officers. The last Capetians and the first Valois thus heralded Loyseau, for whom the most worthy service was not "the call of arms but civil service to the state", the nobleman *par excellence* no longer being the warrior but the magistrate. If this feeling was to be short-lived, it was because of the problem of fiscal exemption which favoured the nobles, a problem which was immediately present once royal fiscality developed. Thus it was the question of fiscal privileges which emphasized with renewed vigour the demarcation line between commoners and noblemen. It was to embitter relations between the second Order and the commoners, both magistrates and merchants, but this bitterness was to become very marked only in the early modern period. As for the other commoners, artisans or country folk, it was the very principle of taxation which was to cause them such long-lasting dissatisfaction, far more than the principle of fiscal exemption for the nobles.

Medieval revolts cannot be catalogued as conflicts of Orders. The second part of the present work will show that 'horizontal solidarity' goes very little way towards explaining medieval rebellions; neither can they be explained as a clash between one Order and another. One finds, on the other hand, many examples of a 'vertical solidarity' between the members of one single geographical grouping, made up of very different strata and orders: from this point of view as from others, the uprisings of the seventeenth century do not have any different characteristics from those of the fourteenth or fifteenth centuries.

Marginals, common people and the elite

V. Pareto went beyond the notion of a society formed of multiple groups when he distinguished in the social body only two 'classes', the elite and the non-elite. He had found this to be true of every society. If one abandons the term 'class', which was evidently not taken by Pareto in the Marxist sense, one can say that, for him, a society is divided into two parts only. Contemporary sociologists have modified this partition and arrived at a tripartite division; they distinguish between the elite (below p. 63), the common people, namely all those individuals who have a place in society without having any 'directive' role, and the marginals, who are often very poor and who, above all, feel themselves to be outside the framework of respected society.

This tripartite division is useful since it goes some way towards explaining at least one aspect of the rebellions. The case of the elite is of such importance that it merits a separate examination and thus will be the subject of the next chapter; there remain the two other cases. Their study will show that there is nothing in the division which is in contradiction to the society of Orders.

(A) The marginals

In a society of Orders, as in any other society, certain groups or certain men, the outcasts, feel, rightly or wrongly, excluded, 'on the margin of society'. This sector forms a most favourable breeding-ground for the eruption of a rebellion.

In these groups, Cohn has seen the main participants of millenarian upheavals. For him, it is no coincidence that the eleventh century marks both the disruption of 'traditional' society through the growth of cultivated areas and towns, and the beginning of a series of apocalyptic revolts: there would seem to be a link of cause-and-effect between these two phenomena. According to him, "the areas in which the age-old prophecies about the Last Days took on a new ... meaning and a new, explosive force were the areas which were becoming seriously over-populated and were involved in a process of rapid economic and social change. Such conditions were to be found now in one area, now in another, for in these respects the development of medieval Europe was anything but uniform".

The traditional way of life of the peasant community probably degenerated at the time of the great material expansion which began in the eleventh century. We can follow Cohn when he tries to understand why the agricultural society of the early Middle Ages seems to have been relatively unreceptive to militant eschatology: at that time, "to an extent which can hardly be exaggerated, peasant life was shaped and sustained by custom and communal routine". The family community was extremely strong in fact, and the manorial regime, even if it was harsh, provided relative security even for the serfs (at least those who were beneficed vassals) because tenure was already most often hereditary by right. If the ties of blood and neighbourship "bound, they also supported every individual", just like the authority of the lord. Thus, "the network of social relationships into which a peasant was born was so strong and was taken so much for granted that it precluded any very radical disorientation". Certainly, the social, religious and economic horizons were geographically very narrow, contact with the world beyond the boundaries of the *villa*, later the manor, being rare, if not non-existent: produce was exchanged with the peasants of neighbouring domains; one went to the local market, seldom further. The relative immobility of the rural world would have made the very thought of a fundamental transformation of society "scarcely conceivable".

From the eleventh century onwards, there was no longer a question of immobility or resistance to change. The new agricultural lands and their new centres of population were due to the collaboration of the lords with peasants who became tenant-farmers. The peasants (serfs or otherwise) had often come from elsewhere, even if from only a few kilometers away, as was generally the case. Without going into Darwinism, one has to accept that there were some peasants who profited neither from the better living conditions which were, after some years, the lot of the landlords, nor from the improvement in the lot of the tenant-farmers of the old estates. And without going as far as Pirenne, one has to recognize the existence of rootless groups, and especially of rootless individuals, some of whom finished up in the town where life, since it was different, might seem more bearable from a distance (the urban 'proletariat' of the nineteenth century onwards was also rural in its origin – it could not have been otherwise). Another mobile group were the youngest of over-large families, the 'youth', who were willing to take any sort of employment, to hire their sword to any prince, as they travelled Christendom. Finally, although the growing population of the West found life much better, on the whole, from the eleventh century onwards, there were men who lived "in a state of chronic insecurity", as a result of too rapid a rise in the population. These were the peasants without land who had become agricultural day-labourers, and certain town workers who could easily become a prey to complete disorientation. And let us not forget the presence, at least at the end of the Middle Ages, of the urban unemployed. Even artisans – masters and, more frequently, journeymen – could, at a time of diminished economic activity, find themselves worse off than the tenant-farmers of the surrounding countryside. In addition, the textile industry making goods for export was, in particular, often dominated by important merchants whom one can, from the thirteenth century onwards, if not before, term precapitalists: they were able to reduce a badly paid and overworked labour force to despair, any dissenter being dismissed and condemned to a long period of unemployment.

The economic expansion does not seem to have absorbed the entire surplus population for long, hence the rapid multiplication of beggars, even in small towns. They were willing to hire themselves out as mercenaries or to swell the number of malcontents, no longer satisfied, as they had been when fewer in number, with asking the monks for alms. The good poor (amongst them the Cistercians, in the early days, then the mendicant friars from the beginning of the thirteenth century onwards) began to be contrasted with the bad poor, those who were reproached, rightly or wrongly, for their idleness and vices. In the thirteenth century, Guillaume de Saint-Amour and St Bonaventure were to say that their poverty only came from their idleness or their wickedness, poverty being harmful to the social order and a scandal.

Cohn has examined only the area between the North Sea, the Rhine and the Somme, but his views can be applied to almost the entire West, with the probable exception of the backward countries. Peasants without land or with too little land to support them, beggars, vagabonds, day-labourers and unskilled workers, the unemployed – they are to be found even in a period of economic prosperity – journeymen with an uncertain future, without a stable and recognized status, living "in a state of chronic frustration and anxiety, formed the most impulsive and unstable elements in medieval society". Any disturbing, frightening or exciting event, anything which "disrupted the normal routine of social life" acted on them with an extreme sharpness and provoked very violent reactions. Their reflex was frequently to form themselves into salvationist groups under the aegis of men whom they believed to be saints. Some of these groups, from the eleventh century, were faithful to the Church. There were many. But others departed from orthodoxy, or else the Church expelled them (sometimes for political reasons): they were actuated primarily by the landless, as is shown by Jean Musy for the eleventh and twelfth centuries in France. While the salvationist movements which had remained within the Church often took part in the building of a cathedral or just a church, and united men and women of all conditions with the aim of forming a 'holy people' (see, for example, the account of Aimo the Norman for the middle of the twelfth century), the movements formed by the surplus or marginal populations acted quite differently.

These movements tended to prefer their leaders to have come from outside, although they did not want them to be rootless individuals. The leader imposed himself as a holy man, or better still, if he were sufficiently eloquent, as a saviour and prophet. He would claim to be in possession of revelations from God and he would assign to his disciples whom he had turned into fanatics "a communal mission of vast dimensions and world-shaking importance". Faith in this mission, the assurance of being divinely appointed to carry out prodigious tasks provided these disorientated men, deceived by life and society, with hopes which transfigured them. At last they had a place in the world, they even felt themselves to be an elite, infinitely superior to the rest of mankind, thanks to the miraculous powers of their leader. And their mission was to end with the radical transformation of the society which had excluded them: eschatological myths were perfectly adapted to their needs and to their innermost desires. But, in order to change society, it was necessary to strike the wicked, to make them expiate the suffering which they had inflicted on the 'holy', the outcasts. Then, with the world purified, the Kingdom of the Saints, governed by their Messiah, would be attained: comfort, security and power would at last come to them, and for all eternity.

Thus, those on the margin of society could move from a passive to an active role under the influence (frequently interconnected) of an increase in misery on the one hand – such as that brought about by the plagues at the end of the Middle Ages – and the emergence of a messiah on the other. Flight, silent rejection, individual acts of disengagement or protest were superseded by revolt. This can be seen particularly clearly in those cases where vagabonds became suddenly and violently restless: when they did, there was an outburst of aggression.

We cannot entirely agree with Jean Baechler when he includes in the number of active marginal groups peasants in revolt and rebels from amongst the commonalty. Some marginals may well have been found amongst these two groups, especially amongst the urban commonalty, but it should be noted that rebellion tended to be provoked and nourished by those peasants who were quite well-off in normal times or even in times of famine. Similarly, in the towns (in Italy, for example) urban disturbances were readily led by men who did not figure among the most underprivileged. We are no longer dealing with millenarianism; it is no longer a question of anti-societies or, if it is, it is to a very slight degree only. Besides the predominantly millenarian revolts, the only movements which can be thought of as anti-societies (that is marginal groups who fundamentally reject society) were movements of outcasts active in the countryside during wars. These included the companies, brigands and ecorcheurs of the Hundred Years War whose mixture of vagabonds, peasants *and nobles* were guilty of so many outrages. In these highway bands there was quite a sizeable proportion of nobility, often the lesser nobility. The frequency of their presence demonstrates that the anti-societies could encompass, besides the marginals, representatives of very different social strata. Thus we have additional proof of the absence of any conflict of Orders, *a fortiori* of 'class' conflict – even in the fifteenth century when these groups proliferated.

(B) The common people

The common people, which includes all those who are not marginals and who do not belong to the elite, represents the vast majority of any given population. Since a revolt, like a revolution later, is the deed of only a small number of the whole population, it follows that the people as such has never been totally comprised of, or even included in its majority, men of revolt or, later, revolutionaries. To say that 'the people' revolted does not generally mean much; neither on the scale of a country, which would be a pointless hypothesis for the Middle Ages, nor even on the scale of a region, the case of medieval Italian towns being a particular exception: Florence, for example, at the time of the Revolt of the Ciompi, where for a period marginals and common people sided together. Moreover, the people is not homogeneous, it is not one complete whole. Its most classic division into peasants and townsmen corresponds to a fact, a fact which is sometimes obscured but to which Chayanov rightly drew attention. In 1925 he had first shown Marx's mistake in wanting to apply to the agricultural world his reasonings based on an examination of the Manchester proletariat: peasant society is an autonomous society, obeying its own laws as a result of the "over-lapping between family and business". This imbrication might have existed in the Middle Ages in the urban working classes, but it was infinitely less evident than in the peasant milieu.

(1) The peasants. The lack of documentation about the early Middle Ages makes it very difficult to distinguish the different strata which might have gone to make up the rural world at that time. We have only scant knowledge of the true status of the serfs and we do not really know how great the difference was between freemen and serfs. Besides, the economic level of both remains shrouded in mystery. Certainly, from Carolingian polyptychs one can see that the tenements were of variable size, on a scale from 1 to 50, the biggest not always exceeding ten hectares. It is often concluded that the peasants of the early Middle Ages formed a more or less homogeneous mass, but this is perhaps only a result of deficient information.

From the eleventh century, and especially from the thirteenth, the old distinction between freemen and serfs which had become vague and pointless with the growing (if not general) decrease of serfdom, gave way to a clearer differentiation: it was claimed that there were several peasant strata. Which one or which ones were a possible fermenting ground for revolts?

Village people, 'low' people as Loyseau was to write, were considered in the seventeenth century as being higher in the social hierarchy than artisans and other tradesmen. Research has not yet advanced far enough for us to be able to tell if this was already the case between the thirteenth and sixteenth centuries. Be that as it may, "a man always belongs to several social groups and it is necessary for the understanding of revolts to specify the part played by peasants in two territorial communities, the village and the seigneury" (Mousnier).

The village was part of the Church since it was a parish. Its land, on the other hand, formed a lordship, or was part of several if, as frequently happened, several lords shared it. The three Orders were thus usually represented in a village. Many nobles, we know, were country people living usually on their lands, and were to remain so as long as war or civil service to the king or prince did not keep them away for long periods. Even when this was the case, and it happened more and more frequently in France after 1300, the lords did not leave the land and simply live off their income from it, as Marc Bloch's outmoded and erroneous theory would have. The birth and growth of tenant farming for the cultivation of the reserve were to signal neither a withdrawal from the land nor a break in sentimental attachment. As the village was often the most important place in the parish, it would have a parish priest, and there could well be monks – a prior at least – in the neighbourhood. From the end of the Middle Ages in the northern countries, earlier in the South, the large villages had a notary or scrivener. And there were artisans in these villages, too, their numbers growing from the eleventh century onwards: cartwrights, shoeing-smiths, carpenters, masons, wet coopers (in wine-growing regions), etc. But the bulk of the population was made up of those who worked the land. Here we must distinguish, at least from the eleventh century onwards, several strata which remained in existence well beyond 1500 and the difference between which seems to have been economic more than anything. The tillage farmers (*laboureurs*) were the peasants *par excellence*, not so much because they had the most ground as because they had the means of buying and maintaining a strip of land. The day-labourers (*manouvriers*) and manual workers (*brassiers*) come at the other end of the peasant ladder: having only their house as tenement and the plot where it stood, plus just one field or a small adjacent vineyard, they could survive only by using the 'commons' and waste land for grazing and by hiring their services to the farmers and the lord. Between these two peasant categories there stood an intermediate category made up of peasants who, for want of a better term, are called 'middle-ranking': in good years their tenements allowed them to live quite well because they had a contract for stock-rearing, but extra work was essential to them in bad years at least.

Historians rarely agree as to how the numbers in these three categories increased between the thirteenth century and the 1500s. They do agree, on the other hand, that up until 1250 the population grew more rapidly than the area of land under cultivation: the tenements thus became smaller and the standard of living of the peasants, excepting about half a dozen in each village, deteriorated. This half-dozen were the most affluent and those amongst whom the lords mainly recruited their officers and tax-farmers, in other words the *coqs de village*. The reason for historians' lack of agreement in other areas of this question is obvious: the numerous difficulties which arose in the fourteenth century and the first half of the fifteenth resulted, for some historians, in an improvement in the lot of the 'middle-ranking' peasants and the day-labourers whilst, according to others, the events profited only a small group which was already favoured and whose circumstances thus improved even further.

The influence of the richest farmers was undoubtedly strong in the village, even if it was exercised only through the intermediary of the village assembly, an institution which had resulted from the growth in communal activities during the great centuries of the medieval period. The villagers now began to possess commons and they drew up rules for the right to use these under the direction of the lord's agents, men frequently taken from among the village leaders who thus became the middle-men between the tenant-farmers and the lords. The assembly elected its representatives who were increasingly involved in the apportioning of different taxes, notably the royal or princely taxes when they appeared and also, and frequently, the seignorial tallage or other taxes due to the lord. If there was to be, for example, a communal shepherd, the rich farmers had a decisive say in choosing him. And so on: all matters of common interest, including the rotation of crops when it started in the later centuries of the Middle Ages, were, if not always controlled, at least always influenced by the highest peasant stratum. The same was true of the parish: the churchwardens were frequently chosen from this stratum. In short, after the lord, it was the village leaders who exerted a preponderant influence, all the more so since they could offer work and rent some of their lands to other peasants from whom, when they became tax-farmers, thus after 1250 (earlier in England), they levied seignorial taxes leased with the reserve lands.

The beginnings of a class society in the country can be seen here. But they were timid beginnings, and went no further for the moment. In any case, Jean Baechler is right in saying that "the people never constitute a concrete universality" since it is composed "of different social groups whose interests may be, and generally are, divergent". This same sociologist notes judiciously that "the struggles between well-to-do peasants or tenant-farmers and poor peasants or manual workers took up more energy than struggles against the lords; a similarity can be seen in the conflict between skilled and manual workers in the nineteenth century, for example in the United States". The idea of constituting the people, of both town and country, into one "objective and subjective entity, the proletariat or working class, corresponds perhaps to a prophetic vision of the future but cannot be in the least confirmed by looking at the present or the past". And, contrary to an opinion which is still very widespread, it was not the poorest peasants who generally furnished the main and most active participants in the revolts. And again, it was principally the richer areas such as the Ile-de-France (in its wealthiest sectors), Flanders and the Rhine valley and so on, not the poor regions, which experienced rebellion.

(2) The town commonalty. (In what follows we exclude the marginals from this term.) Just as in the country, several strata can be distinguished amongst the common people of the town. Rivalry between trades and between master artisans was often more frequent and more bitter than that between masters and journeymen or varlets. This was so up to the end of the thirteenth century particularly. Then the situation changed: 'horizontal' rivalry did not cease, it even became more bitter as a result of the economic difficulties which induced keen urban protectionism, yet 'vertical' conflicts were henceforth to be more frequent and more serious. More clearly than in the country, the beginnings of a class society were becoming evident in the towns in the third Order.

Vertical solidarity was, in principle, strengthened by urban exclusivism and the tightening of each trade's monopoly because of the economic difficulties and, even more so, by the fact that the trades, or some of them, were beginning to have a say in 'economic politics'. This was true at least of that solidarity which linked the well-to-do artisans and those who were less well-off. But, as Pirenne has brilliantly shown, the notion of common good gave way to that of the particular good of each group, the producer completely sacrificing the consumer, higher wages for the workers and higher prices for the masters becoming the prime aims. Vertical solidarity is henceforth *against*: thus, all the artisans of the big Flemish towns united against the textile industry of the small towns and the country in an attempt to ruin it; or all the burgesses in a town – those of the commonalty as well as the patriciate – agreed on restricting, in an often draconian manner, the right to become a burgess. But 'vertical' solidarity was often limited, unless the clienteles of important families were involved, to this negative aspect.

On the contrary, horizontal solidarity became stronger almost everywhere. As there was a wish to safeguard acquired positions, everything had to be used to prevent the most skilful and the most competent from eliminating their unfortunate or less gifted fellows: the number of varlets and apprentices employed by each master was fixed at its maximum and the raw material was to be strictly divided between the masters. And most trades were closed at the top, thereby preventing any circulation of the elites: at the end of the fourteenth century, access to the mastership was usually stringently regulated – the new practice of the *chef d'oeuvre* and the raising of the entrance tax for a mastership were means of ensuring that only the sons of masters could gain a mastership. To be sure, this was not always the case and even when the statutes seemed hostile to any circulation of the elites and to any social promotion, there is proof that journeymen were sometimes able to become masters. All the same, the general refusal to promote was a latent threat which could only embitter relations between the masters and their journeymen and apprentices. That, more perhaps than the economic and monetary troubles, explains the great number of social conflicts, strikes, dismissals of the intractable and the obstinate. Although not a general phenomenon, and one should not attempt to see in it any sign of class conflict, one notes the creation of associations formed only of journeymen – and this was something quite new. At first, the wage-earners of the same trade formed 'temporary coalitions' to wrest wage increases from the masters. But reaction was not long in coming: clauses were added to the statutes which gave the jurists of the trade the right to fix wages and to settle all conflict between a master and his workers, unless this right was exercised by the urban authorities, which remained under the domination of the important merchants. It was exceedingly rare to see the birth of 'parity commissions' such as those created in Strasbourg in 1363.

Later, the workers, who had thus not found, exceptions apart, any support from their superiors, created their own permanent groups. These were the fraternities (*compagnonnages*), camouflaged as religious or charitable brotherhoods, which obliged all the journeymen to belong to a group, levying a tax on them (in order to create a fund or *boîte*) and imposed strong discipline on them. All this was necessary to be able to bargain with the masters of the trade from a position of strength. Some fraternities, those of the most important trades, thus those of the textile industry, achieved good results. In the towns concerned the urban authority felt it wise to urge the masters to make concessions. It is certain that an improvement in the lot of the apprentices and varlets followed fairly often, although it is difficult to judge the extent.

Formed at first on a local level, the guilds of neighbouring towns united and, more and more as 1500 drew near, some associations achieved a radius of action which was regional, even inter-regional. The explanation, although one wonders whether it is a satisfactory one, could lie in the fact that from the end of the fourteenth century social movements spread easily.

The fact remains, nevertheless, that urban disturbances or revolts of the end of the Middle Ages cannot be totally explained – far from it – by a confrontation between masters, solidly supporting one another, and members. The intrigues of the clienteles – as is clearly seen in Florence in 1378 – and those of politics continued to occupy an important place. And there were to be many cases where vertical solidarity suddenly found its old strength to the detriment of revitalized horizontal solidarity. Whatever the case, one section of the commonalty, but not always the same, was represented in the urban revolts, whether as an activating force in the revolt or, as happened even more often, as a manipulated tactical force.

CHAPTER 4

The preponderance of elites in rebellions

We shall restrict the meaning of the term 'elite' to denote mainly the most active members of the highest strata in the social hierarchy. We thus depart somewhat from Pareto's view that elites are to be found at all levels of society.

As we understand them, the elites are heterogeneous, something which Marx did not see when he called them the "owning class", a class forming a homogeneous, united whole. It is, in fact, their very heterogeneity which accounts for some rebellions. In many others the elites play a large part, although they may not seem to at first sight; this is because they know how to use marginals and, especially, the common people, in the furtherance of their own ends. These ends are sometimes conservative but are never steeped in despair, which is why we avoid using the word revolt as a synonym for certain disturbances.

Responsibility of the elites in rebellions

(A) Definition of elites

In general, the elite does not form a concrete universal any more than the common people. Studies of it owe much to the sociologist V. Pareto, who has made it easier for us to see in what ways it is similar or dissimilar to the ruling class (because it is the owning class) which is seen by Marx in every non-communist society.

One might say, as a first approximation, that the elite is composed of those individuals who have the greatest power and prestige, in other words, wealth. But Vilfredo Pareto put forward a wider definition: "Let us suppose that in all areas of human activity each individual is given a mark which indicates his ability, something like the way marks are given in examinations. For example, someone who excels in his profession gets 10. Someone who only manages to have one solitary client is given 1, so that 0 is reserved for somebody really hopeless. And so on for all areas of activity . . .." Thus the elite is made up of those who, by their natural gifts or their industriousness etc., are more successful than the average and to whom 10 can be given. The notion has a qualitative value, for it is not simply a question of material supremacy. And there is a possible elite in all social milieus: for Pareto, the successful swindler, the popular poet and the self-made man come within the definition. However, we shall leave to one side, at least for the moment, the elites of the lower strata (*coqs de village*, messiahs and 'saints'): see below, p. 70.

Those who belong to the elite are the 'superior' members of society, and Pareto divides them into two groups: those who, directly or otherwise, have a role in government (the governing elite) and the others who form the non-political yet directive elite. Thus it is better to use 'elite' in the plural. Depending on different civilizations the elites have been made up of the clergy, warriors, entrepreneurs, state officials, etc. – all categories which had been recognized as elites in the Middle Ages.

The elites are stratified and hierarchical – indeed, Mosca even saw a super-elite within the elite: this nucleus would be formed of a small number of individuals or families who enjoyed the greatest power and influence. And Mosca, for example, proposes that it is not class conflict which is the moving force and complete explanation of history, but the elites with their ideas and interests. For if the elite is stratified, that means that there is not just *one* 'class', as Marx would have it, standing in opposition to the 'common people' and the marginals. There is no homogenous group which is at once dominant and directive, which has a virtual monopoly over the law of ownership and which controls production and exchange as well as the state. Society is more complex.

In each unit (whether castellany, principality or kingdom – or township) there is a *political* group. Its members generally belong to the directive and to the dominant groups, but by no means always. If it is true that in the Italian cities – Venice, Genoa, and particularly Florence – those who dominate the economy (the bourgeois bankers, textile manufacturers, maritime businessmen, etc.) control politics, it is far from always being true elsewhere. This can be seen in the case of the Parisian merchant bourgeoisie, the majority of whose representatives, having no official posts, had no part in directing royal policy and administration, and so were not a royally-appointed directive elite, but rather an economy-dominating elite. The subordination of 'politicians' to businessmen is thus only true for the Italian cities (and also the Hanse towns). It is much less marked in the Low Countries, for example, where political difficulties resulted on several occasions precisely from a conflict between the intentions of the count of Flanders, to mention but one example, and the intentions of the burghers. Economic power was then – and is still quite frequently – only a strong determinant, not a sufficient force, in politics.

The effective exercise of control is the criterion of the directive strata. The criterion of the dominant strata is, primarily, social standing, which does not come solely from economic strength. The men whom we have provisionally termed *notables* in our discussion of France at the end of the Middle Ages enjoyed a determinant social position: they belonged both to the directive and dominant elites, whilst the big merchants belonged only to the latter. For there is some distance between economic superiority and effective command: a bailiff or royal official with little land, makes commands in the name of the king and carries more weight with society in the end than the owner of handsome fiefs or a fine business, who has no access to executive power. Moreover, even in modern societies, it is not the owners who necessarily have real power: in 'capitalist' countries as in 'socialist' countries, it is really techno-bureaucracy which dominates. This began, although quite unobtrusively, the moment royal or princely power was far enough advanced to give birth to 'offices', to a structured administration, thus around the thirteenth century, sometimes earlier (in England, for example), sometimes later. But it would be anachronistic to take the notables for true technocrats. And nobles and burghers, even those who did not belong to the body of 'officials', held their places within several strata of elites. But for this we must consider the circulation of elites.

(B) Rebellion and the circulation of elites

The circulation of elites is both a sociological and historical problem and, being one of the major problems of social mobility, is closely linked to situations of potential unrest.

Marx came very close to the idea of a circulation of elites when he wrote in *Capital*: "The more capable a ruling class is of absorbing the best men of the oppressed class, the more solid it is and the more dangerous its reign." Or when he noted that in the United States "the classes . . . are not stabilized, they exchange and transfer elements in a constant flux". For him, of course, the whole notion was linked to the means of production of the time. But Marx never went very far along this path, for it conflicted with his idea of class which was, by definition, one solid whole. Now the idea that, through the fluidity which social mobility supposes, the circulation of elites constantly modifies social differentiation and stratification (although according to a variable rhythm), is of prime importance: for example, a society of Orders in no way implies the solidification of the strata which go to make it up. According to Monnerot, Marx ascribed to the exploiting 'bourgeoisie' and the exploited proletariat of his time, "a degree of crystallization which in fact belonged to the old Orders or estates". But if an Order is in principle crystallized, which is not yet the case before 1500, it does not mean to say that membership of that Order is always hereditary: membership of an Order is lost, and is acquired, as Mousnier reminds us.

"The absence of hope in the short or medium term was an integral part of Marx's view of the proletariat" (Monnerot), but even if Marx had been right in respect of his own period, was this always the case with people belonging to the lowest strata? Social mobility certainly created a *de facto* solidarity between the lower and upper strata; it allows only a slight degree of 'class consciousness'. The existence of 'class' differences between children who have climbed a rung of the social ladder and their parents contradicts the Marxist notion of 'class': it is wrong to speak, as sometimes happens, of class conflict when one is dealing with clashes between generations.

In principle, social disturbances arise in extreme cases, that is to say, either when there is no circulation of elites or after a violent acceleration of the circulation. For, the more active and durable social mobility is, the less risk there is of conflict between strata. But is this mobility, as far as the elites are concerned, a conspicuous feature of the Middle Ages? If so, did it have sudden bursts of activity, comparable to those associated with the revolutions of later periods? As Mousnier has shown for seventeenth-century revolts, social mobility is undeniably a prerequisite for the eruption of a disturbance: one group wishes to improve its 'classification' in the social ladder and thus urges rebellion. But mobility, in this case, prevents the rebellion from developing into a revolution whereas a static society, on the other hand, has been able since the eighteenth century to provoke revolution.

Society in the period from the eleventh to the thirteenth centuries does not appear to have been a static society at the level of the elites any more than it was in the seventeenth century.

Until the eleventh century it is evident that elites were to be found only among the clergy and the aristocracy. The Church was always a very important means of circulation for the elites in the Middle Ages: lowly people, including serfs, were able to become abbots, bishops, even popes, though the aristocracy probably provided the Church with most of its dignitaries. And new men have always been able to infiltrate aristocratic families, adventurers attracted by the military calling, ambitious men of various origins. On the other hand, one cannot speak of peasant elites, still less of a circulation of elites in the peasant milieu: those who rose in station were relatively few in number, and when they did, they left the peasant world, for example to enter the Church.

Things changed with the eleventh century, and in several ways. Firstly because some well-to-do and fortunate peasants rose above the peasant mass but without leaving the peasant world. It is impossible to specify if there was already any circulation of elites at this level. As for the clergy, nothing very new happened: circulation there generally remained quite active. In contrast, the problem of the partial re-invigoration of the nobility is posed in fairly new terms. Above all, there appeared new elites which formed the upper level of the 'bourgeoisie' which had come into being with the rise of the towns. The circulation of elites then speeded up, but was it violent enough to cause grave disturbances, as grave, at least, as historians (even non-Marxist ones) have believed?

(C) Disturbances in the circulation of elites

Completely static societies are rare. Even those of the early Middle Ages cannot be said to have been completely so. On the other hand, societies where the circulation of elites is restricted are very common. When this is the case, it is futile to suppose some conspiracy among the elites: it is just that an individual has more chances of obtaining a high mark, as Pareto would put it, if he has come from a more favoured milieu, a certain tendency towards heredity having become evident in the societies of Orders – the same is seen in modern-day techno-bureaucratic societies. Moreover, every social system tends, by its very nature, to be self-perpetuating and new conditions, not necessarily economic ones, are needed for the circulation to be disturbed and modified.

The chess-board of the opposing social forces can be considerably transformed by the appearance of new social forces, as was seen by Baechler, who singles out just three examples in history: the bourgeoisie in the eleventh to the thirteenth centuries, the workers in the nineteenth century and the youth of the twentieth century. The development in the number and power of the towns during the eleventh to the thirteenth centuries, and the consequent appearance and growth of the number of 'bourgeois' (there were bourgeois before the formation of the 'bourgeoisie') posed many social problems in new terms. Pirenne perhaps exaggerated the extent to which these bourgeois seemed almost abnormal beings to the elite of feudal society, but feudal law and its judges were little in tune with the requirements of business and trade, which are different from those of the land.

Marxists such as P. Vilar have rightly noted that the bourgeois structures of the Middle Ages have nothing in common with those of the nineteenth-century capitalist bourgeoisie because of the collective nature of urban life at that time, something which is also found in the merchant world (cf. the guilds). As the towns depended on one or several lords, disputes had to go before the seignorial authority and the 'innovations' moreover sometimes seemed frightening to the lord, especially the ecclesiastical lord who, unlike the lay lord, lived in the town (except in the south of France and Italy). The hatred which is supposed to have existed between the bourgeois and the lords was neither a frequent nor a long-lasting phenomenon. It was the historians of the first half of the nineteenth century (1789 was not far away . . .) who had a false vision of a conflict which they saw as being centuries old and insurmountable. This was a characteristic 'ideological' illusion which Marx adopted in the way we know so well.

Moreover, the 'bourgeoisie' did not remain a unified body for long (was it ever one in fact?): the powerful bourgeois who dominated the town economically, who often took control of its administration and who sometimes exploited the finances, were soon to be more or less opposed by the *commonalty* (after they had separated themselves from them). Stated in these terms, this opposition is rather crude for there were often, in fact, more than two strata at the heart of the medieval bourgeoisie. In any event, the upper stratum became an elite, an elite whose members did not clash so often with the members of the noble elites (consider the case of the French *notables*). This shows that the emergence of new elites does not necessarily lead to disturbances: a feeling of solidarity between two elites of different origins can be very quickly generated, developed and preserved. Although the nobles retained a keen awareness of their superiority in prestige, their contempt for the bourgeois was neither as strong nor as frequent as some, such as Bloch, for example, have thought: for such historians, the nobility closed ranks precisely because, with its own resources dwindling, it believed itself threatened by the new wealth of the bourgeoisie; in fact, if, especially during the thirteenth century, some noble fortunes foundered, the impoverishment of knights was by no means general. And the nobility never really closed ranks entirely; there were bourgeois who joined its numbers in every century. Yet again, historians have been too carried away by Etienne Marcel's 'revolution'.

Nevertheless, in Paris in Marcel's time, as in other towns at the close of the Middle Ages, there were serious conflicts between bourgeois and noble elites. Now a splitting-up of the elites is one of the conditions for the outbreak of a disturbance. The problem is one of elites which are divided at a governmental level, the finest example of which occurred in 1789. If one of the elites wins the support of some of the common people it can gain victory and some victories were, in fact, won even before the end of the Middle Ages, but these were generally short-lived. There is, in these cases, no such thing as a really 'popular' rebellion, unless individuals from the commonalty succeed in outflanking the members of the attacking elite. But the elite can, on the other hand, have responsibilities in movements which, either apparently or in reality, seem truly 'popular': this was often the case, particularly in the Italian towns.

Is it possible for the common people to stage a rebellion against the elites? We know that the *people*, in general, do not form a united whole because of the great diversification brought about by the division of labour and by differences in ways of life, environment and mentalities. The common people can only rise as one in a very narrow political 'unit', as in the case of the *city-states* of Antiquity and the Middle Ages. What is more frequent is that some of the people burst on to the political scene because some elite or other is paralysed (e.g. the noble elite after the disaster of Poitiers and at the time of Etienne Marcel's revolt) and because another group (for example the merchant bourgeoisie in 1358) needs the support of the people in order to take over the political scene. This is often explained by some abdication of, or void in, the state's authority.

The revolt of the Ciompi (1378) illustrates another constant in the history of relations between the elites and the other social strata. There is a constitution or reconstitution of a common front between the elites and the *commonalty* each time the *rabble*, the marginals, become too threatening or too strong. At first, revolt could indeed unite the rabble and at least some of the common people (the minor artisans in Florence) but later, when they were weary of the disturbances and violence, the people broke away from the marginals and sided with the elites. This is particularly frequent at a time of messianic revolts, but is not too infrequent in those revolts which are predominantly social or political.

Whatever the category of revolt under consideration, one should seek to understand the state of the elites, their immediate problems, their relations with each of the commonalty groups and the relationships between the different elite groups themselves. Even in those rebellions which fully deserve, in principle, to be called *popular*, the members of the elite, or simply some of them, whether or not they are isolated in the heart of their milieu, are not necessarily threatened by the revolt. They have either been involved in stirring it up, or they will profit from it, whether it succeeds or not. The elites rarely go against 'the current of history'.

Any single social stratum, belonging to the elites or not, can be the agent of a rebellion. But 'revolutionary predestination' does not exist either. Yet the leading role remains, directly or indirectly, with the elites in many types of disturbances.

Responsibility of individuals in the rebellions

Ellul believes "more in the importance of the human presence than in that of the deeds themselves as an immediately decisive factor in a revolt once a favourable situation obtains" – which is quite correct. Yet it is not only due to the influence of Marxism that the leaders and the most important followers have been too frequently neglected. This neglect was also a reaction against the victims of revolts (later, of revolutions) who would have liked to explain everything as a conspiracy led by a few individuals.

By definition, if we take, on this occasion, the term elite in the widest sense given it by Pareto, all leaders are members of an elite, including those of humble extraction. Their first disciples would belong to the elite, too. Or indeed – and one rarely thinks of this – these men took themselves to be an elite, perhaps wrongly (consider the case of the messianic 'saints').

(A) Social origins of the leaders

Since, in rebellions, vertical solidarity is often a more decisive force than horizontal solidarity, the leaders of disturbances can be recruited from any social stratum.

Some 'leaders' – or men whom one thinks of as such after reading contemporary accounts – came from the lower strata of the town or country. They are fewer in number than was claimed under the influence of Engels who, in his *Peasant War in Germany*, gives it to be understood that, like the other leaders, Thomas Münzer, a "plebeian revolutionary" of the 1520s, was the victim of grave social injustices: in fact, "he was born not ... to poverty but to modest comfort; and his father was not hanged by a feudal tyrant but died in bed in the fulness of years" (Cohn).

The list of laymen of modest beginnings is not very long. We can name Peter de Coninck, leader or head (for some historians there is a difference between the two, the second implying a more elevated position and greater consistency in outlook) of the Bruges uprising of 1300: according to the *Chronique artésienne*, he was "of poor family; and was a weaver, and for weaving ... had never had 10 lb. to call his own". Another example would be the carder, Michele di Lando, in the Florence of 1378; or for rural revolts, Guillaume Cale, 'captain' of the Jacques of the Ile-de-France in 1358, and Wat Tyler, leader of the 1381 English uprising. And it is not easy to believe that these two men, and others too, came from the most humble levels of the peasantry. Guillaume Cale was well-educated (it seems he might even have had a sort of chancery and he certainly had a seal), and this "learned and eloquent man" showed military qualities and experience which could only have been acquired in the army; he was not one of Mello's poorest peasants. The same could be said of Wat Tyler. Apart from these names, only a few others emerge, such as those of the well-to-do peasants Nicolas Zannekin and Jacques Peyte at the time of the 1323–1328 rebellion in maritime Flanders.

It is true that the somewhat better-known names of humbly born clerics should be added to the above. There is a tendency to see in them "eloquent mouthpieces" of the *common people* and the insurgents. But this is only partly true. They were able, in fact, to spark off disturbances by their preaching. A number of 'messiahs' were naturally recruited from their ranks: there is but a narrow margin separating orthodoxy and the moral condemnation of the wicked rich from the heresies announcing the reign of the saints and the extermination of all the rich. Even in the Church, the pope and his bishops were not always agreed on where this margin should begin and end. Thus, in 1077, a Cambrai cleric, Ramirdhus, incited the weavers against the frivolity of the clergy and its simony. The result was a rebellion, brutally put down by the bishop who had the cleric burned as a heretic. But Gregory VII, who used certain movements of religious exasperation to further his reforms (J. Musy), was to proclaim him a martyr. Later, the Church was nearly always unanimous in its fixing of the bounds of orthodoxy.

It is sometimes difficult to know whether some holy hermit turned leader of insurgents was indeed a cleric: 'King Tafur', head of a band of Provençal crusaders at the end of the eleventh century, perhaps lived an ascetic life, but rumour had it that he was a Norman knight who had given up arms to don the sackcloth. It is not easy to distinguish the part played by the 'marginals' from that of the 'popular' clerics: who really was the ascetic who passed himself off as Baudouin in Flanders in 1224–1225? Was he an impostor or an enlightened soul? On the other hand, we are sure that the men who adopted, in particular, the theses of Joachim of Fiore (1145–1202), whose influence was to last until Marxism, really were monks. Through Joachimism, popular preachers could pass imperceptibly from traditional sermons to calls to revolt.

In any case, the two most famous leaders to have come from amongst the clergy are certainly John Ball and the Czech, Prokop the Great. The latter became a real war leader. As for the former, he inherited a long tradition from the English preachers. They, like their contemporaries on the continent, had for a long time been accustomed to setting the stamp of shame on the sins of all the social strata, reserving their sharpest barbs, however, for the rich and powerful. Furthermore, since the thirteenth century, the interpretation of the Last Judgement as the day of vengeance of the poor had been enormously popular in England. In his guide for preachers, the chancellor of Cambridge University, John Bromyard, gave a model sermon on the Last Day. It was certainly not a call to revolt, but an exhortation to the rich to behave well towards the poor and an exhortation to the poor to calm their rancour by thinking of the divine reward. The chancellor nevertheless summarized in no uncertain terms the grievances of the lowly folk against the great. As Cohn points out, "All that was required in order to turn such a prophecy into revolutionary propaganda of the most explosive kind was to bring the Day of Judgement nearer – to show it not as happening in some remote and indefinite future but as already at hand". This is exactly what John Ball did in a sermon attributed to him: the prophecy is about to be fulfilled and the common people, as the children of the Kingdom, are summoned to carry out without any more delay the complete destruction of demonic powers which will announce the arrival of the millennium. The authenticity of the sermons, like that of the obscure oracular verse, attributed to John Ball is by no means certain, but the basic content is certainly the same as that used by him for rousing the crowds. In Londoners "envious of the rich and the nobility" (according to Froissart), he awakened an impatient anticipation of the 'final struggle' (an expression which thus existed long before Eugène Pottier . . .) between the poor, 'God's cohort', and their oppressors, Satan's soldiers. For John Ball, the millennium would not just be the kingdom of saints as foretold by traditional eschatology, it would also mean a return to an egalitarian state of nature, hence the lines taken from the sermon on 13 June 1381 which had such repercussions:

> When Adam delved and Eve span,
> Who was then a gentleman?

We notice that the role of clerics as instigators or leaders of revolts springs from two factors: their influence over the people through their sermons; the revival of the old myths which were still lying dormant in the popular mentality. And one is tempted to compare these clerics with Hitler: the same magnetic oratory, the same ability to re-awaken ancient myths among the people who were quite ready to accept them precisely because they still smouldered away under the surface; this was something of which these priests, in communion with the simple minds, were keenly aware. About forty years later, the Taborite priests in Bohemia were to act and speak in exactly the same way as John Ball.

If one maintains that there does, in fact, exist a 'class front' against the humble and weak, one evidently cannot imagine representatives of the upper strata playing this role, unless we think of them as the Russian intelligentsia before and during the 1917 Revolution; the intelligentsia was thought to 'represent' the proletariat, adopting its aspirations and placing itself at its head. This idea of 'representation' might well be just a sophism or, at the very least, obscure the fact that some of the common people or the marginals are, at such a time, only a tactical force used by those who supposedly 'represent' them.

Many important bourgeois – important through social prestige or simply through wealth – are to be found at the origins of medieval furores and involved in their development. The following are the most typical or best-known cases. That, first of all, of the Arteveldes, James and Philip, his son. James, a well-to-do fuller who, through an insurrection, found himself at the head of the town of Ghent, apparently felt only contempt for the journeymen in the textile industry. We know that he died in July 1345, a victim of the weavers: the hostility between weavers and fullers (the latter being supervised by the weavers because of the division of labour) was constant and was not, moreover, in any sense a 'class conflict'. In 1381, Philip, the son, was put at the head of a new Ghent rebellion. It was not because of a 'democratic spirit' that he relied on the humble in his management of the uprising, but because he needed a tactical force. His death at Roosebeke on 27 November 1382 in no way rang the knell of a democratic venture. The second case is that of Etienne Marcel who could not be said, any more than the Arteveldes, to be lacking in skill or political know-how. This merchant provost – and the power of the Parisian merchants is well known – was hardly an insignificant person: through his mother he was descended from royal officers, but what distinguished him most was his paternal ancestry, made up of drapers and money-changers (these powerful money-changers had not yet abandoned their *banks* to solicit for high finance offices . . .). So he was a very important businessman who, in addition, because of his duties, had supreme control over every commercial activity in Paris. But he was also an embittered man: he thought he had been badly provided for in the partition of the Marcel inheritance and he did not get on with his second wife's family, the powerful des Essarts. So we have a very powerful man, rich in spite of everything, but who considers himself wronged. One should not go too far in this direction, but it is certain that some leaders became leaders precisely because they were embittered, rightly or wrongly, against their own milieu. But embittered does not necessarily mean *déclassé*, there is a big difference. In any case, by a sort of compensatory phenomenon, the bitterness develops ambition and the taste for demagogy. For, more so than others perhaps, the leaders of rebellions who have come from the upper strata show themselves inclined to demagogy. So it was with Salvestro de' Medici. In 1378 when he entered the Florentine *signoria* at the start of the movement which was to culminate shortly afterwards in the Revolt of the Ciompi, the Medici family, if not yet at the height of its power, was already very influential, like other families, moreover, such as the Strozzi family, of which one member, Alberto, was going to side with the rioters. Thus, in Salvestro, we have a very important bourgeois who is sure of a clientele recruited from the widest of milieus, ranging from merchants to humble craftsmen and the poor, and who is applauded for his wish to rid the city of "the evil tyranny of the great and powerful". The varied make-up of his supporters is an excellent illustration of the strength of vertical solidarity between bosses, artisans and workers. And finally, the last case, that not of a man but of a group, the butchers. The financial power, although not the prestige, of the butchers in the towns from at least 1300 onwards has long been noted, as well as their important role in the most 'popular' urban movements. Take Paris, for example. Everyone knows of Caboche who gave his name to a real period of terror in 1413. In the French capital, as elsewhere, the butchers had control over a whole horde of varlets, notably the flayers or skinners. Yet Caboche, no more than Capeluche, "flayer of men", was not really a leader. He would seem to have been rather an instrument manipulated by John the Fearless.

The nobles who placed themselves at the head of 'terrors' or subsequently directed them once others had set them in motion, cannot, any more than the bourgeois leaders, all be classified as embittered, disappointed in their ambitions for social advancement. They were not all demagogues either. But, except in Italy, they were better able to employ vertical and personal solidarity than the bourgeois, profiting from the lasting strength of the bonds which united them with their peasants. And, because they were more in contact with the popular mentality, they were more sensitive than the bourgeois to messianic myths.

One of the first eschatological movements to be reasonably well known, that of the 1140s, had as its leader a nobleman, Eudes de l'Etoile, a native of Loudéac in Brittany. He was the youngest of his family, thus one of those young men who, as G. Duby has shown, formed in the West in the eleventh and twelfth centuries groups ready for any adventure because they had had to leave the over-populated ancestral home whose lands could not support all the head of the family's children. As one of the count of Flanders' notaries, Tanchelm, had done thirty years earlier at Antwerp, he proclaimed himself the Son of God and his power to fascinate quickly attracted disciples to him. His movement established its bases in the Breton forests, before spreading out as far as Gascony. Whilst his hordes, who moved about with speed, desecrated churches and committed massacre, Eudes, like Tanchelm before him, led a merry life surrounded by a sumptuous court. In spite of his carousals, his prestige was long-lasting: when the pope's legate came to Nantes to preach against the *heresy*, the population paid no heed. In the end, Eudes was taken prisoner in 1148. He died in the prison to which he had been condemned. His disciples, who refused to deny him, were burned as heretics.

A greater number of nobles were leaders of other kinds of movements, principally rural revolts. In the rising in maritime Flanders (1323–1328), the head of the insurgents' army was an important country lord, Guillaume de Deken, who even became burgomaster of Bruges once the townsmen had reinforced the country rebels. Pirenne has shown conclusively that it was not a question, in this case, of a real *Jacquerie*. But it is precisely in real Jacqueries that the presence of noble leaders is conspicuous. Were there really no nobles in the Jacquerie of the Beauvaisis and the Ile-de-France in 1358, usually seen as being explicitly hostile to the nobles? Was it an exception? Must we follow Froissart blindly in his repeated insistence on the hostility of the Jacques to the nobles in 1358? Indeed the monk of Saint-Denis, author of the *Grandes chroniques de France*, is not so dogmatic: "and in these assemblies there were mostly working men, but there were also rich men, burghers *and others*". Siméon Luce interpreted these lines as possible proof that "members of the nobility" were present amongst the insurgents. Whatever was really the case in the French 'terrors' of 1358, the involvement of nobles with the rebel English leaders of 1381 or with their seconds-in-command is certain. Just because some manorial documents were burned (as happened on the *grande île*), it does not necessarily mean that the revolt was directed totally against the nobles. As a leader, we can cite Bertram Wilmington of Kent. As a very active second-in-command, we can quote Roger Bacon, a knight who, together with other nobles, had himself enrolled as lieutenant by another leader, Geoffrey Litster, a dyer. But, in the fifteenth century, we shall find more evidence for our argument: the groups of *brigands* who roamed several French provinces which were occupied by the English, consisted both of peasants and men-at-arms, and they nearly always had nobles for their leaders. In fact, these *brigands* were not always highwaymen but were frequently men made desperate by the English presence and motivated by a nascent national feeling. The peasants were quite happy to recognize their lords as leaders both in revolts and, outside the framework of the country seigneury, in 'nationalistic' movements.

(B) Qualities of the leaders

All the social strata have thus provided the insurgents with leaders. In every strata we find men who have been leaders, and others who have been led. What were the qualities, the characteristics of these leaders?

A desperate situation or a surprising and unexpected event – or indeed both at the same time – provide the spur for the outbreak of a revolt. Now the leaders are the *spur* in certain cases (for in others, the leaders appear only during the revolt, whose secondary causes are due to a general crystallized feeling, not individual incitement). What they have to say "provokes awareness and gives expression to what has been slowly maturing" (Ellul). Thus Guillaume Cale was, for the *Chroniqueur des quatre premiers Valois*, a "learned and eloquent man". It is not just by chance that, well before 1789, the leaders who emerged in France at the time of meetings of the States General were often good orators, efficient, and well knew how to command attention and obedience, such as Etienne Marcel or one of his allies, Robert le Coq, bishop of Laon, another ambitious man who was inconsolable at not having become chancellor of France. Similarly in Italy, leaders like Cola di Rienzo in Rome, in 1347, possessed great personal charm and great powers of oratory. And chroniclers have handed down to us the essentials of various leaders' speeches. An eyewitness, Alamanno Acciaiuoli, one of the Florentine priors in 1378, noted the quite theatrical – not to mention demagogical – attitude and speech of Salvestro de' Medici before the council, a speech which was at the root of the riot. He also noted how his seconds-in-command went about things; one was a member of the great Alberti family, who assembled the people from a window of the council chamber. One of the qualities necessary in a leader, besides the gift of oratory, is precisely the ability to choose his seconds-in-command well. That holds good for all categories of revolt, but for the 'messiahs' the gift of powerful (and in this case inspired) speech is even more necessary.

At least from the eleventh century onwards, and even more so towards the end of the Middle Ages, the presence of rootless individuals, of marginals, made a call to insurgents possible and immediately effective. Mousnier, especially, has drawn attention to this for the early modern period, but it was already true of preceding centuries: the bands of vagabonds and 'brigands' (in the usual sense) who roamed the countryside and congested the towns, already operating under the leadership of a minor local head whose personality created the "group bond", supplied the leader with his first troops. And it is not often that one finds true leaders who were not at the same time military leaders with organizing ability. Otherwise there would just have been riots rather than revolts. For it was necessary to impose a modicum of discipline on the first groups, then to recruit new supporters, something quite easy in itself, and finally to lead the men into combat, whether in street or open country.

This is what happened with the likes of Guillaume Cale and the Taborite leaders. Otherwise there would have been an unruly mob soon committing massacre, as was the case, for example, in certain 'popular' crusades.

Organizing ability was thus necessary. But with many leaders, even amongst the most remarkable, this seems to have been limited to the violent riot. There were exceptions: if the Jacques were defeated in 1358 at Mello, it was partly due to the absence of Cale, treacherously trapped the previous day by Charles the Bad and taken prisoner. If he had been there the battle might well have had a different outcome. And several other leaders also had a certain sense of reality, an awareness of the need for overall organization. But their political inspiration seems to have been weak, with the exception of Wat Tyler and the Taborites. Precisely because they were insurgents looking towards the past and a return to the 'good old ways', it would be wrong to interpret arguments put forward for rousing and fanaticizing the crowds as stated political ideas. Even when Etienne Marcel, a man of higher stature than most leaders, went to the French towns – and not only Paris – as the champion of urban liberty, was he, as the nineteenth century believed, fired by a vision of the future or was he simply nostalgic for a past in which the monarchy was not yet in control of its towns? Was he really sorry that St Louis had subjugated the towns, due partly to the scandalous oppression of the commonalty by important families? Or was it simply a ploy of the moment in order to unite the bourgeois of the other towns against the regent?

On the other hand, Tyler and the Taborite leaders really do seem to have mingled visions of the future with the hotch-potch of eschatological ideas. This was perhaps also true of Peter de Coninck and the two Arteveldes, even though their attempts to extend the rebellion throughout Flanders were possibly, as in the case of Etienne Marcel, only a means of recruiting new supporters at all costs. But one cannot make any firm general pronouncement on this since, sooner or later, a revolt would peter out, usually in a blood-bath, and since, the Taborites excepted, the leaders did not have time to prove themselves as political leaders. All hypotheses are possible, which explains why historians can hold contradictory views. The fact remains, however, that the insurgents and their leaders have always been more ready to look towards the past and that their programme – when they and one – was aimed at a return to the golden age or the age of the 'good old ways'. Nowadays one would say that they were almost all 'reactionaries'. But they knew how to sense and use the rancour and grievances of the different strata without, however, proposing many realistic remedies. To transform revolt into revolution by giving it a theoretical basis was the aim of Wat Tyler only, and perhaps of a few Taborite leaders too.

When a leader dies and there is no one to take over from him, a movement collapses almost immediately. Ellul insists quite rightly on the *negative* role of the leader as being more important than his *positive* role. For the "creative and provocative role of the leader is a matter of chance". As a revolt develops, the leader sees his own importance grow. But the fall is brutal. The death of Guillaume Cale was perhaps almost as much the cause of the collapse of the Jacquerie as the setting-up of the Contre-Jacquerie by the nobles. An even better illustration is the 1381 Peasants' Revolt, which died the very day after its leader had been killed.

PART II   A TYPOLOGY OF THE REBELLIONS

We here venture to make the first attempt at categorizing those medieval rebellions which have not been lost without trace. We are able to consider only the major rebellions and our conclusions are necessarily provisional as we await the publication of new works which we would hope to have gone some way towards encouraging.

Most rebellions seem very complex in their motivation, changing character during their development even when they are particularly short-lived and thus even more poorly documented. The principle of this typology has been to seek out in each specific case the dominant characteristic or characteristics: one peasant disturbance may thus be classed as millenarian while another may be in a different category because the millenarianism of the second is weak compared with that of the first. The same revolt has been mentioned more than once only in exceptional cases.

Our tripartite typology – messianic movements, rebellions connected with the problems of social mobility or the circulation of elites, revolts bound up with crisis situations – is a totally undogmatic attempt at clarifying a very complex matter.

It goes without saying that the motivation behind a revolt is not necessarily the only factor to examine in our classification which must also give important consideration to the strata involved in each movement.

CHAPTER 1

Messianic movements

As well as having apocalyptic backgrounds, the messianic movements which culminated in riots or uprisings are alike in having been almost the only medieval *terrors* to display anti-society characteristics. They were "radical forms of opposition to order", since their supporters wanted to leave the established order and enter a new society advocating a new order and new values, with everything the total opposite of the old order. As was to be seen in the twentieth century with totalitarian movements, ideology and internal organization form coherent wholes: the anti-society is a clearly defined alternative. But in the Middle Ages there was never any rational analysis of the relationships between the opposing forces nor any sufficiently effective strategy for the seizing of power. In this sense, there was no 'revolutionary' anti-society in the Middle Ages.

There is another characteristic. Rebellions of this kind have been known since the eleventh century, and more was known about them at first than about other kinds. Is this solely due to the hazards of documentation? Contemporaries were perhaps more interested in them because they appealed more to the imagination. And since these disturbances (which were to have sequels right up to our own period) brought into play ancient myths, it is possible that for this reason they were the first to assert themselves. Although the proportion of 'marginals' was particularly high amongst the agents of these rebellions, many other social strata were often represented amongst them too. It should also be noted that the leaders – often *messiahs* – are better known than the leaders of other categories of revolt: they made a greater impression on public opinion.

The popular crusades

Despite the statements of various chroniclers, it is by no means certain that there was a truly messianic movement around the year 1000: in any case, if there was one, it did not degenerate into a rebellion. What is certain, on the other hand, is that in some places movements changed into millenarian revolts from the time of the first crusades in which the 'poor' took part.

There has been speculation as to whether the crusades, quite 'extraordinary' enterprises, could not be explained in part by plagues and marvels, the former having been very numerous and long-lasting, so it was said, in the eleventh century. But one should always beware of chroniclers who, even when they have no apocalyptic ulterior motives, misuse tales of disasters and marvels. It was in the eleventh century that serious famines became less frequent since it was at this time that waste lands were beginning to be cultivated. Thus Raoul Glaber's writings, in which the millenarian legend appears, cannot be taken literally. What is indisputable, on the other hand, is the influence on the populace of the preaching of hermits, particularly that of Robert d'Arbrissel's disciples in Anjou. Through their sermons, the people were aware of the disasters befalling Christians in the East well before Urban II came to France. And they were made even more aware of events by former pilgrims exiled from the East, who went about begging with other poor people, recounting – and exaggerating – their troubles as they did so, as well as those of the Christians who had stayed where they were after the terrible Turkish advance. This led to a strong resurgence of the old myths. The legend of the King of the Last Days enjoyed great vogue once again, as is shown by Adson's *Libellus de Antichristo*. Under the influence of the memory of Charlemagne it was modified, and the emperor was made the precursor of the crusade. Urban II himself would seem to have believed that Charlemagne went to fight the pagans in the East. The use literature made of this increasingly widespread belief is, of course, well known. The *Pèlerinage de Charlemagne à Jérusalem*, which predates the First Crusade, seems to have turned the first Frankish emperor into a messiah.

This messianism, in an orthodox doctrinal form, can be seen quite clearly in Urban II's speech at Clermont. Antichrist is going to come, so the pope is said to have announced, and Christians should hasten to seize the Holy Land where they will be tried and conquered but will finally triumph. Those who went would be the *chosen ones*. The time which was drawing near should be prepared for if, through Christians, "the might of the pagans is to be overcome and if, as the prophets foretold, Christianity is to be re-established in Jerusalem before the coming of Antichrist . . . . so that the king of all evil, who is to have his throne there, may find in Jerusalem the bodily might of the faith to which he is so opposed". Like other invasions which posed a more direct threat to Christianity, the Turkish advance acted as a spur to orthodox messianic ideas; its effect on heterodox ideas was even greater.

Millenarian beliefs were making a great impression on the people at this time. Behind the first departures for the East there was "a chaos of emotions", "relics of ancient local religions, a return of old pagan myths which were mixed pell-mell with the myths of the rebirth of the world, popular Christian eschatology, rudimentary theology and moral ideas of the Eastern world in order to form the crusade's religion" (A. Dupront).

Following the Clermont appeal in 1095 which was addressed to everybody, "rich and poor", whatever rank they belonged to, "knights as well as peasants", many preachers began calling the Christian people to deliver Christ's tomb which had fallen into the hands of the infidels. Among these men there were bishops and simple clerics, but also individuals who had not received any clear official authorization from the Church. And it was these latter who attracted most *pauperes* : some passed themselves off as prophets, easily acquiring the prestige which the poorer classes readily accorded ascetics and performers of 'miracles'. The most famous of these, or rather, the only one known, was Peter the Hermit and, like the other *prophetae*, he was both a preacher and leader of a company. The masterly portrait which Guibert de Nogent painted of him is well known. He went about barefoot, ate as little as possible and knew how to galvanize the masses, who went as far as to pull hairs from his donkey to keep as relics . . .. His success was thus immense. It was so great that in northern France an army of poor people who had sold off their few meagre possessions in order to buy weapons and have some ready money to take with them, set off with him as their leader as early as March 1096, four months before the 'official' crusade was ready. He advanced into the Empire at the head of a horde – his enemies would say a mob – while other *prophets* formed other 'armies' in Flanders and the Rhine Valley and elsewhere. Faced with the difficulties of the time, which were probably no more serious than they had been twenty years earlier, people had for some years been gathering into penitential groups around *holy men* in order to seek salvation together. It is clear that the appearance of *prophetae* was bound to swell the numbers of these salvationist groups. With often whole families going – women and children on carts as far as possible – they saw their numbers increased by other poor peasants or lowly townsmen. But adventurers, renegade monks, in short vagabonds, also joined in with the 'true' *pauperes.*

For the *poor,* the crusade did not have exactly the same meaning as it did for Urban II. The fate of the Christians in the East really mattered little to them; it was the thought of delivering the Saviour's tomb which uplifted their zeal. And the Jerusalem which obsessed them was not just the city which held Christ's tomb, it was charged with all the messianic hopes which had, centuries previously, passed from Palestine into the West and which suddenly took on a new force. For these crusaders the Holy City had a double attraction: that of being the place which had witnessed Christ's Passion, and that of being a land fertile in spiritual *and material* blessings. In short, the earthly Jerusalem of the end of the eleventh century was in some respects extremely close to the City of God for these simple people. This explains their intense exaltation, something which is also found amongst the *pauperes* of the south of France who joined the 'official' army under Raymond of Toulouse.

What is striking is the process of "self-exaltation of the poor" (Cohn) which actuated these Christians. They were the elite of the crusaders, a people chosen by God, whereas the barons had not been chosen. However, we know that most of Peter the Hermit's companions perished on the way. Quite a number nevertheless managed to reach the Holy Land and the most fervent of these, those most under the influence of messianism, then abandoned themselves to excesses: they were given the mysterious name of the Tafurs (= vagabonds?), and the crusade became for them a sort of obligation to massacre the infidels. They were a 'Holy People' over whom reigned a King Tafur – perhaps once a Norman knight: armed only with axes, shovels and boar-spears, in rags and abandoning themselves to pillaging by virtue of the "divine predilection" which authorized their acts, these men believed themselves destined to deliver Jerusalem. And they did in fact take part in its deliverance, but they were held responsible for much of the massacring: as in every messianic movement, the 'saints' had a duty to massacre the 'pagans'. This has applied not only to the Saracens, but also the Jews. Although the knights did not indulge in any pogroms, either in this First Crusade or during later ones, one of the characteristics of all the popular crusades, from the very first one onwards, was a virulent antisemitism. This was how the messianic violence of some *pauperes* first manifested itself: right from the period of preparation and its sermons, Jewish communities had to choose between conversion and extermination, as at Rouen, Speyer and Worms for example. Should this be seen simply as a reflection of the hatred felt by the poor for the rich? This is debatable since poor Jews – but not rich Christians – were killed just the same as the more wealthy Jews. It is, in fact, a clear consequence of the *holy* people's belief in its mission to exterminate the enemies of God wherever they might be. As soon as medieval messianism became openly apparent, it showed its propensity towards violence: it was a charitable deed to kill those non-Christians who had refused to be converted.

This violently antisemitic aspect was to be retained by future apocalyptic movements, as for example those of the other popular crusades (1146–47, 1197, 1212, 1251, etc.) where there were increasing numbers of 'children'.

However, since all these attempts by the 'children' and the 'poor' failed and as the return journeys were disastrous, contemporaries saw hovering over all the guile of Satan: God was not with the crusaders. They also saw in these crusades, and this has not always been made clear, something which disturbed the order willed by God as well as the order desired by the well-off and those in high positions. On the other hand, in popular piety a sort of 'exaltation of the child' is seen: witness the celebration of the Festival of the Innocents or that of the Children which, much later, the Council of Basel was to condemn, as it did the Festival of Fools. At the same time in folklore, especially Germanic folklore, legends grew up evoking the magic power of child charmers. Finally, shepherds and shepherdesses were to play a primary role in the popular imagination and even in art (note the many *Adorations of Shepherds* and *Nativities*) until the end of the Middle Ages and beyond.

The *Pastoureaux* affair, in 1251, marks a certain turning-point. In future, as Cohn has justly noted, messianic movements of the masses were going to become "more frankly hostile to the rich" because the number of *marginals* in the towns was increasing. The glorification of poverty – a term which was no longer given its exact evangelical meaning in eschatology – was going to lead to a complete condemnation of wealth: the rich could now only be wicked rich. For the chiliastic movements, they were henceforth irrevocably condemned and damned. St Thomas Aquinas, followed by the entire Church, none the less reaffirmed the doctrine of the Fathers of the Church: God has given each man his station and though the rich man ought to give alms, he ought to do so, however, in such a way that he and his family may live in a manner fitting to their station. The idea that wealth could be well used is something which messianism considered impossible from about 1250; after the Saracens, the Jews and the clerics, the rich were endowed with demonic qualities. The rich man had become an Antichrist. "In the minds of the apocalyptic sectarians ..., the rich layman was already undergoing the metamorphosis which in course of time was to transform him into the capitalist of twentieth-century propaganda: a being truly demonic in its destructiveness, its cruelty, its gross sensuality, its capacity to deceive and, above all, its near-omnipotence" (Cohn). The last crusades of the *pauperes* were the sign of a new millenarianism in Europe, "... which aimed, however confusedly, at casting down the mighty and raising up the poor".

All this is clearly seen at the beginning of the fourteenth century. Thus, in 1309, a year of famine in the north of France and part of the Rhine Valley, a new crusade arose. Its members styled themselves *pauperes* but there were nobles amongst them too, not just peasants and artisans; this demonstrates that social factors are not the most influential in these sorts of movements. They were armed and lived off alms and pillaging, killing Jews and attacking châteaux. But when they laid their hands on the property of the duke of Brabant, who three years previously had routed an uprising of cloth-workers, they were crushed. Then everything started up again in 1315, a year of high prices and famine which perhaps seemed to indicate the start of a serious economic crisis. Chiliastic hopes became extremely strong once again and whole processions of penitents sprang up. Prophecies foretelling a blood-bath and the massacre of the clergy and the powerful were rife. Meanwhile, in 1320, Philip V proposed a new expedition to the East despite the pope's scepticism.

The people, firmly under the influence of messianism, needed little persuasion from the preachers, two of whom, in northern France, were unfrocked clerics. The sermons had an immediate and tremendous success and the movement apparently spread with the speed of a "whirlwind". Once again young shepherds, beggars and vagabonds banded together, set off and saw their ranks swell. Their leaders had, as was customary, proclaimed themselves God's messengers. Some 'crusaders' were put in prison for fear of a renewed outbreak of trouble. But one horde succeeded in reaching Paris and besieging the Châtelet before making their way towards the Plantagenet south-west of France where the Jews, expelled in 1306 by the Capetians, had found refuge. There was once again looting of Jewish houses and slaying of Israelites, this time in Bordeaux as well as in Capetian towns, such as Toulouse and Albi, from which not all the Jews had been expelled. Blame was heaped on the priests, too, "those false shepherds". In Avignon, a papal residence, and almost everywhere in the south of France panic seized the population who rushed to close the gates of their towns; some crusaders began to die of starvation. Then, on the pope's command, the seneschal of Beaucaire hunted down the new *Pastoureaux* and imprisoned them or had them hanged. The survivors went to Aragon to persecute the Jews there until they were dispersed by the king's son. This violent uprising had certainly come to be seen as a threat to the very structures of Christian civilization.

The movements of 'impostors'

Although they did not have the same import and repercussions as the millenarian crusades, chiliastic movements were active in some regions at about the same time. An impostor would suddenly appear claiming to be a lost personage.

The first to be tolerably well-known was the pseudo-Baudouin. Soon after his election as emperor of Constantinople, the count of Flanders, Baudouin IX, was captured and killed by the Bulgarians. His daughter, Jeanne, succeeded him in Flanders and we know the difficulties she had with Philip Augustus. When the people learned of the death of the French king, there was considerable unrest which helped towards the resurgence of a fairly old myth, that of the Sleeping Emperor. This was an offshoot of the myth of the Emperor of the Last Days, which had been modified through becoming firmly associated with the prestigious memory of Charlemagne: legend had it that the first Carolingian emperor was simply sleeping in his shrine at Aachen waiting for the time when he would reappear among men to overthrow Saracen tyranny and initiate the era of felicity which was to precede the end of the world.

Baudouin IX's extraordinary adventure made him seem a fabulous character in the popular imagination: he was not dead either, but was merely discharging a penance imposed on him by the pope. He was alive and disguised as a beggar, but his atonement was almost completed and he would soon reappear in his glory to liberate the Flemish. Now in 1224, near Tournai, a tall hermit with a "flowing beard" was seen. And it was soon maintained that he was none other than Count Baudouin. In any case he quickly surrounded himself with a group of advisers and was visited by nobles and by a nephew of Baudouin's who believed he recognized him, or at least claimed he did. The followers of this 'messiah' were clearly not all *pauperes*.

In April 1225 the inhabitants of Valenciennes went to seek him out in his forest and brought him back carried in triumph and clothed in scarlet. The majority of the Flemish and Hainaut burghers and nobles were quick to allow him to assume power, putting no difficulties in his way: the sceptical Countess Jeanne was considered a rebellious daughter and, in addition, a slave of the Capetians; political ulterior motives and millenarianism thus went well together. The hermit, at the head of the insurgents, took up arms against Jeanne: it was yet another war of religious exaltation, a crusade. Held by more and more to be a saint and crowned with great ceremony as count of Flanders and Hainaut in May 1225, the pseudo-Baudouin began to take on the external appearance of the Emperor of the Last Days. People flocked to meet him, and all the social strata took part in this collective exaltation, including the clergy, although weavers and fullers were his keenest supporters. But every-thing quickly crumbled: received by Louis VIII at Péronne, the pseudo-Baudouin was identified as a poor Burgundian peasant, Bertrand de Ray, minstrel and charlatan. Unmasked, he fled to Valenciennes where the common people rose against the rich burghers, the latter having just lost their faith in this 'messiah'. The French besieged the town and the impostor fled but, once recaptured, he was imprisoned and hanged at Lille after seven months' usurpation of the titles of count and emperor. At the foot of the gallows, he confessed – and this is important – that it was knights and burghers who had led him astray. In short, the humbler classes had done no more than follow. However, his memory would remain alive amongst the 'commonalty', who believed he was merely asleep and awaited his awakening, "as the Bretons await King Arthur". Thus there was a prolonged period of restlessness, sometimes under the surface but sometimes more explicit, which, along with other factors, contributed to so many movements of unrest in the Low Countries for one and a half centuries (Pirenne).

Until the thirteenth century eschatology was derived from ancient pagan myths and Johannine and Sibylline prophecies. But a new form of eschatology was born in the thirteenth century; it led an independent existence at first before being absorbed into the first swell of events on which it was to have a very great influence. This new form, which lasted till the early modern period, originated in the writings of a Calabrian hermit, Joachim of Fiore (died 1202): an inspiration would seem to have revealed to him that the scriptures had a hidden prophetic meaning. In itself this was not something completely new; the Fathers of the Church had already asked themselves whether the Bible could not be interpreted in several ways, but their motives were purely moral and dogmatic. This time, however, it was a question of seeking in the two testaments a means of understanding and, above all, of forecasting history: the key to the scriptures had apparently been revealed to Joachim of Fiore; it was the *Evangelium aeternum* which, according to the Apocalypse, will be preached in the last days of the world.

History was seen as an ascent through three states. The first, that of the Father, of the Law, being that of the Old Testament; the second, that of the Son being the state governed by the New Testament; and the third, that of the Holy Spirit, would mark the apogee of mankind's history on earth. The Old Testament was the age of fear and servitude, the New is the age of faith. Finally, with the third will come Love, Liberty and Joy. It will be the Kingdom of Saints which will endure until the Last Judgement, God's knowledge penetrating even lost men as they devote themselves to mystical contemplation. Nothing of this being *a priori* heretical, popes were to go as far as to encourage Joachim to write down his visions. But, in fact, this third state of earthly history contradicted the Augustinian view according to which, after Christ's coming to Earth, the Kingdom of God had been realized, as far as is possible in this world, with the birth of the Church, and no other divine kingdom should, nor could, succeed it. *Nolens volens*, through his predictions Joachim of Fiore became associated with the myth of the Golden Age: despite appearances which had even deceived popes, his doctrine was clearly a millenarian one which his followers were to distort more and more, giving it increasingly heterodox, anticlerical and ultimately quite profane meanings. It has even been stated that social mythology has never lost the memory of the three Joachite states. And Cohn has noted that "Horrified though the unworldly mystic would have been to see it happen, it is unmistakably the Joachite phantasy of the three ages that reappeared in, for instance, the theories of historical evolution expounded by the German Idealist philosophers Lessing, Schelling, Fichte and to some extent Hegel; in Auguste Comte's idea of history as an ascent from the theological through the metaphysical up to the scientific phase; and again in the Marxian dialectic of the three stages of primitive communism, class society and a final communism which is to be the realm of freedom . . .. And it is no less true – if even more paradoxical – that the phrase 'the third Reich', first coined in 1923 by the publicist Moeller van den Bruck and later adopted as a name for that 'new order' which was supposed to last a thousand years, would have had but little emotional significance if the phantasy of a third and most glorious dispensation had not, over the centuries, entered into the common stock of European social mythology".

In the thirteenth century, people were particularly sensitive to the Joachite forecast of the final transformation of the world, which was to be preceded by an inevitable *period of incubation*. The period between the birth of Christ and the coming of the Third Age was to last forty-two generations, that is, the same number as had passed between the time of Abraham and that of Christ. Forty-two multiplied by thirty would equal about twelve centuries: the culmination of history was thus to be between 1200 and 1260. Meanwhile, it was vital to prepare the way; this would be the responsibility of a new monastic order charged with preaching the new gospel throughout the world. Twelve patriarchs would convert the Jews. A *novus dux* would force mankind away from the love of worldly things and would inspire it with the love of God. In any case, before the start of the Third Age, Antichrist would have to reign for three and a half years, chastising and destroying the corrupt Church. But his fall would come and with it the Age of the Holy Spirit.

These were explosive predictions as was clearly apparent when that wing of the Friars Minor which was the most faithful to St Francis' ideal of poverty formed a group known as the Spirituals: it was they who spread abroad the writings of Joachim of Fiore and added apocrypha. The Spirituals very quickly came to regard themselves as the new religious order foretold by Joachim of Fiore, an order which would replace the Church of Rome and guide mankind towards the Age of the Holy Spirit. It goes without saying that the apocalyptic ideas drawn from Joachism were successful first and foremost in Italy. But extremist groups went much further than the Spirituals. A rebel chiliasm flourished in the wake of Cola di Rienzo and Fra Dolcino. Cola di Rienzo's adventure in Rome is well known, but not always its motivation. It had political causes (the *captivity in Babylon*, in other words the pope's sojourn at Avignon) and economic causes (difficulties of this kind were frequent in the Eternal City), not forgetting the continual excesses and disorders provoked by the warring of noble factions which were tearing themselves apart. But all that does not explain the root of the matter. Nostalgia for the Roman Republic played its part because it was linked to the myth of the Golden Age and, even more, to the Joachite messianism with which Cola di Rienzo was strongly fired. "One of the people, the people's advocate", someone has said. That may well be, but his success was principally because the humbler Roman classes were a prey to chiliasm. Moreover, burghers and minor nobles also supported this man who was at once

sincere and demagogical, pragmatic and visionary..., especially
visionary. Was it hatred of the nobility which made him assume its
honours and titles? To claim so would be very risky indeed. In any event,
his violent ways themselves finally disgusted those of his followers who
had come from modest milieus, and he was assassinated in October 1354.

Outside Italy, Joachism did not have to wait for the end of the
thirteenth century before achieving success, particularly in the Empire:
the role of the *novus dux* who would chastise the Church in the Last Days,
already played elsewhere by Tanchelm, Eudes de l'Etoile and Jacob of
Hungary, was filled in Germany itself by the emperor. The death of
Frederick I (Barbarossa) during the Third Crusade in 1190, lent itself very
well to exploitation by social mythology. Prophecies very quickly spread
through the Empire foretelling that a new emperor, the Emperor of the
Last Days, would soon resume his work, liberating the Holy Sepulchre
and clearing the way for the millennium. These prophecies were later to
be applied to his grandson, the genial but strange Frederick II. For the
first time in the history of the myth, it seems, it was stated unreservedly
that the Emperor of the Last Days would be someone who already held
the title of emperor. We recall that, in spite of the pope's opposition,
Frederick II left for the crusade – although excommunicated – and that in
principle he regained, through negotiation, it is true, with the Saracens,
the Holy Places which had been lost to Christianity for some decades.
Possessed of a charisma which fascinated his age and sowing the seeds of
unrest amongst his contemporaries through his bitter struggle with the
papacy (itself bent on his ruin), he was certainly the man best able to
embody the myth. Several times excommunicated, he reached the point
of threatening to strip the Church of its possessions, the source of its
corruption. There is nothing surprising then in the fact that, in 1240, a
pseudo-Joachite commentary should have seen in him the spirit whose
task it was to chastise the Church before the imminent realization of the
Age of the Holy Spirit, in other words, the *novus dux*. Others, such as the
Spirituals, on the other hand, saw in him the Beast of the Apocalypse.
But, thanks partly to his own prestige amongst the commonalty, partly to
the prestige of the myth, and partly to itinerant preachers, it was the term
novus dux which was most often applied to him. Like Baudouin before
him, Frederick II was thought of by many popular groups as the saviour of
the poor. Writings bear witness to this, as does the history of several
towns, such as Halle: a wind of mythico-social revolt was thus blowing
over Germany at the time of the new phase in the struggle between the
sacerdotium and imperium.

Frederick, through his premature death in 1250, marked the end of imperial aspirations and awakened a nostalgia for a powerful and respected Empire. The Italians were delivered from Antichrist, but the Germans were losing their *novus dux*. A rumour started and spread saying that he was still alive: the pope had exiled him to the East where, disguised as a pilgrim, he was carrying out a long penance. An alternative claim was that he had been swallowed up in the crater of Mt Etna, considered the seat of Hell by some, the refuge of departed heroes by others. Frederick, as the new Sleeping Emperor, was to reappear one day as saviour. And indeed, the year 1260, a critical time in the visions of Joachim of Fiore, witnessed the appearance of an impostor who attracted a crowd of disciples in the vicinity of Etna until 1262. Other new Fredericks were to appear in the course of time to attract and rouse the people. Thus, in 1264, a former hermit from the Worms region passed himself off as the emperor, while about the same time another impostor was the cause of great enthusiasm at Lübeck, but both disappeared even before they were unmasked.

Twenty years later, a megalomaniac established his 'court' at Neuss and his fame spread as far as Italy. He was the Friend of the Poor and succeeded in fanaticizing the urban 'crowds'. Convening an imperial diet at Frankfurt, he summoned Rudolf of Habsburg in order to receive the crown from him. Installed at Wetzlar, this pseudo-Frederick was besieged by Rudolf, who found himself at grips with a fanaticized population. After his arrest and trial he was burned, as only heretics were at that time, because he had proclaimed himself the saviour sent by God to punish the clergy and reign over the world. He had prophesied that he would rise again and his disciples believed him. The consequence was, right up to the middle of the sixteenth century, the appearance of new impostors each time passing themselves off as Frederick risen from the dead and achieving a success proportionate to the restlessness of the time. Thus, in 1348, a terrible year, popular hopes for the return of Frederick, Messiah of the Poor, rose again, as is noted by a certain John of Winterthur. Again, in 1434, the anticipation of this return had lost none of its force. These hopes survived till the beginning of the sixteenth century, as is proved by the writings of an Alsatian, 'the Revolutionary of the Upper Rhine', in which one reads that the way to the millennium is through terror and violence, notably against the clergy and usurers. In the Empire, messianism was thus mixed with a nostalgia for the time when the Empire was a great power, and this is not surprising. But in the writings of the

'Revolutionary', the idea of the supremacy of the German race is also present, as well as almost all the themes which Nazism was later to take up.

Flagellant movements

The practice of self-flagellation which appeared towards the beginning of the eleventh century had, so Christians in the West believed, the virtue of inducing God to avert his rod from them, to forgive them their sins and also to spare them harsher punishments in both this world and the next. Like the *pauperes* of the crusades, the flagellants, who had gradually grouped themselves into sects, saw their penance as imitative of Christ's: flagellation assured the salvation of the flagellant but also of other men; it had an eschatological value.

It was not by chance that the first processions of flagellants took place in Italy, in Perugia first of all, in 1260, the year which was so important in Joachite prophecies. The movement spread like wildfire from Lombardy in the north to Rome in the south. At first it would seem that there was nothing heterodox nor messianic about it: led by priests, the flagellants marched into the towns, beating themselves in front of the churches. To start with, all the social strata were affected but, and this was important for the future, generally it was only the poor who persevered. The warfare between the Guelphs and Ghibellines, insecurity and possibly bad harvests seemed to herald the imminent end of the world and made the coming of the Age of the Holy Spirit more immediate. According to Salimbene, himself more or less a Joachite, the frenzy – heightened by the Ghibelline menace of Manfred, Frederick II's 'successor', whose Montaperto victory seemed to have an eschatological meaning – won even more adepts during the last months of 1260. But, as nothing resembling the end of the world happened, disenchantment spread in the hearts of the Italian flagellants. However, some Italian leaders crossed the Alps and in 1261–62, these flagellants recruited many followers on their way through the towns of southern Germany and the Rhineland. The processions had their own rituals and songs and they are all the more reminiscent of the processions of crusading *pauperes* since the leaders claimed, like Peter the Hermit or the Master of Hungary (the mysterious James or Jacob, leader of the *Pastoureaux* in 1251), that they were in possession of a Heavenly Letter. The text of this one is known and is full of eschatological expressions.

The difference between the flagellants in the Empire and their Italian contemporaries is that the former quickly turned against the Church. The Great Interregnum had revived the messianic nostalgia of the 'marginals' as well as that of the minor artisans, weavers, bootmakers and blacksmiths, etc.; it transformed their group into a "permanent conspiracy against the clergy" which was reproached both for its own defects and for the attitude of the papacy during its conflict with Frederick II. The German flagellants soon proclaimed that they were entitled to obtain their own salvation by themselves and that the very act of taking part in one of their processions absolved a man from all sin. This soon resulted in their being excommunicated, German princes, the duke of Bavaria at their head, helping the Church to carry out its repression. Although banned in 1262, the German movement nevertheless survived, and it was to come out into the open each time a disturbing event occurred, as for example during the 1296 famine in the Rhineland. On the other hand, in Italy and the south of France, the movement remained orthodox and was tolerably well supported by the secular authorities and by the Church itself.

The messianic myth reappears all the more vigorously when a catastrophe is especially brutal and widespread. Nothing could have been more favourable for a strong resurgence, then, than the terrible plague which swept down on almost the entire West in 1348. The plague, even amongst the orthodox, was interpreted as a divine punishment for the sins of the world, and the flagellant processions are explained, although only in part, as an attempt at appeasing God. Rumours announcing the imminent arrival of the pestilence somewhere were generally enough to give rise to processions which were seen as a kind of counter to the epidemic. This practice apparently started in Hungary before the end of 1348 and spread by way of southern Germany towards Westphalia, the Rhine Valley, the Low Countries and northern France. But a group who landed in England were to find themselves up against the indifference of the islanders, although they were also afflicted by the great plague.

In view of the curiously uniform organization of the groups, it seems impossible that their formation should have been entirely spontaneous: the Master or Father, a layman, leading one group was certainly in liaison with other leaders. And the population was very well disposed towards the flagellants: people attended the ceremonies, listened to the songs and speeches and ended up moaning and weeping, with both flagellants and onlookers giving way to collective hysteria. To welcome and protect the flagellants was a holy deed, since these martyrs were atoning for all the sins of the world. Sick people were brought to them to be healed, they were made to exorcize devils and people even believed they could bring back the dead, since some claimed to have seen Christ and the Virgin Mary. It did not take much for the movement to become really hostile to the Church which, it already implied on occasions, one could do without.

It was in 1349 that in Germany and especially the Low Countries, the movement turned towards "a militant and bloodthirsty pursuit of the millennium". Men began to live in expectation of the approaching Parousia and the coming of a warrior-messiah who might well be the Emperor Frederick come back amongst men. The 'radicalization' of the myth corresponded to social modifications within the flagellant groups: the nobles and burghers who had taken part in the beginning often left fairly quickly, the movement afterwards consisting mainly of peasants and artisans. But, as in previous movements, vagabonds and outlaws gradually became mixed in with them, giving the groups an anti-society complexion. And apostate clerics banded together, too. When the pope issued a bull against the flagellants, he depicted them as being mostly simple folk led astray by heretics and, in particular, lapsed monks who should be arrested without delay. Indeed it was often unfrocked clerics who, at least in Germany, set the flagellants against the clergy and the Church.

It must be said too that a *de facto* bond had arisen between some flagellants and Beghards and Beguines, these often being heretics won over to the Free Spirit movement (which probably came into being before the thirteenth century but which had continued spreading almost everywhere, causing the Church much anxiety from the 1300s onwards). Adepts of voluntary poverty and, like all the heretics in the eleventh, twelfth and thirteenth centuries, fundamentally hostile to the rich, they had recruited many followers amongst women and from the midst of the most troubled and distressed elements in the towns. For them, it was right to rob the rich to give to the poor who were necessarily in a state of grace. The Church was thus a prime target.

Having become a widespread messianic movement, and having been reinforced by the adepts of the Free Spirit, themselves possibly organized into a secret society with numerous branches, the Germanic flagellant movement, like that of the *pauperes'* crusades, came into violent conflict with the Church, seized its possessions and maltreated clerics who dared to oppose them, for opposition was inadmissible as far as the messengers of God were concerned. But it was not just priests who were demons, the Jews were too. The widespread massacre of Jews in the West which took place during the great plague was to a large extent due to the flagellants. In Frankfurt, Mainz and Cologne in particular, there was much pillaging and violence, just as in times past. But this time, atrocities were also committed in the Low Countries (in Brussels for example), where the flagellants burned or drowned all the Jews they could find "because they thought that they were pleasing God in that way", according to a contemporary. All this, which happened principally in the last six months of 1349, reduced the numbers of Jewish communities in Germany and the Low Countries and condemned them to segregation and the ghetto.

Did the movement want to cast blame on the other demons, on the rich, so that its members could be an elite of sacrificial redeemers in the full sense? It would seem that some, adepts of the Free Spirit or otherwise, wanted to abolish wealth: the pope testifies to the fact that they became the nightmare of the well-to-do. As in the days of the *Pastoureaux*, their violent anarchism united all the authorities against them. Clement VI, who had shown himself favourable to the flagellant movement in its early stages, was later hostile: in his bull of October 1349, he reproached their followers, in addition to their violent ways, with a number of doctrinal errors, and he called for the suppression of the *sect*. This suppression was not long in coming and threatened the 'masters of error' with the stake.

The movement nevertheless persisted, albeit sporadically, particularly in Thuringia, where a flagellant messiah, Konrad Schmid, helped by successive outbreaks of the plague, roused the people once again. There was insurrection, then repression: in 1368 Konrad, who had also passed himself off as the resurrected Frederick, was burned with six other heretics.

Here and there, in Germany and in Italy, groups of flagellants, whether connected or not with adepts of the Free Spirit, were to reappear, be tracked down and sometimes burned right up to the end of the fifteenth century. And it will be noted that the Peasants' War under Luther was to have its origins near Nordhausen which had been Konrad Schmid's 'capital'. The messianic continuity between the flagellant movements of the Middle Ages and the peasant uprising of Thomas Münzer is obvious: amongst the flagellants there were already not only marginals and artisans but also a fair number of peasants.

Egalitarian millenarianism

In the fourteenth century a society which did not distinguish men according to their status or wealth was no longer thought of as something mythical.

Egalitarianism and eschatological communism go back to Antiquity: the Greeks and Romans bequeathed to the Middle Ages the notion of the 'state of nature', a state in which there is complete equality between all men, a total absence of exploitation or oppression, universal brotherly love and common sharing of women and possessions. The Ancients believed that this state had existed in a Golden Age or 'Reign of Saturn'. This myth, whose place in Ovid's *Metamorphoses* is well known, permeated medieval 'communist' thought; Ovid was familiar to medieval scholars, as was Virgil, who gave pride of place to the legend. And in the second century AD, Lucian put forward an even more egalitarian version of the myth, coupled with a bitter condemnation of his rich contemporaries. The theme belonged to the realm of literature, but also to philosophy, and was found, for example, in the Stoics. The result was that egalitarianism had become a commonplace: human laws had destroyed the divine law of equality and the community order in which mankind had lived happily. However, some Roman Stoics, among them Seneca, differed from the Greeks in thinking that this old egalitarian order was lost for ever: private ownership, servitude, the state, etc., were all necessary because men had become depraved. This was a prefiguration of what the Fathers of the Church were going to write!

Orthodox exegesis thus made use of this Roman myth in applying it to original sin and the fall of Adam, while maintaining at the same time that natural society had been egalitarian, something which many medieval authors were to take up, Beaumanoir among them. At the close of the Middle Ages, many scholastics were still to admit that in society, in its first and best state, there had been no such thing as private property, because all things had belonged to all people. This myth was able to survive for a very long time because the Church made no clear pronouncements to the contrary.

Unlike purely eschatological myths, the myth of the Golden Age could only be introduced to the lower classes by 'intellectuals', mainly the clergy at the close of the Middle Ages. Nevertheless it was a layman, Jean de Meung who, for the first time since Antiquity, re-introduced the myth into literature – and it was into the literature of the vernacular, thus giving him greater access to the people. His *Roman de la Rose* made the Golden

Age and its subsequent decline accessible to large numbers of the laity: this aspect of social mythology is all the more remarkable in that certain elements in Jean de Meung's work were to find an echo in Jean Jacques Rousseau's *Discours sur l'inégalité*.

For the author of the *Roman de la Rose*, the blessed Golden Age ended with the appearance of an army of vices. First of all Poverty and her son Larceny were let loose upon the earth. Anarchy was rife and this forced men to choose someone to restore a modicum of order. But as this prince needed the wherewithal to carry out his task, money was minted and arms were made; worse still, taxes were introduced. Were people now reaching a point where their nostalgia for the mythical Golden Age was being transformed into a desire to recreate it?

The Church has always maintained that a community life dedicated to voluntary poverty was the least imperfect life. But this ideal could only be achieved by a monastic elite, thus a small group and not the majority, because mankind is corrupt. Nevertheless, it had been the wish of some laymen, from the eleventh century onwards, to copy the poverty and the community spirit of the regular clergy and, with or without the sanction of the Church, they formed quasi-monastic communities. Their desire to copy the life-style of the first Christians (such as they saw it at least) could lead to a desire for a return to the Golden Age: the idea of imitating the first Christians, when insufficiently understood, has often led to all sorts of erring ways. Imitating the primitive Church, however, was not enough to make someone be suspected of subscribing to egalitarian ideals. Even the heretical sects which flourished from the twelfth century onwards were not as concerned about economic and social equality as some writers would have us believe. This is particularly true of Catharism and Waldensianism. In short, until the fourteenth century and despite the great success of Jean de Meung's work, heretical movements which sought to re-establish the egalitarian 'state of nature' as it was in the beginning were rare. At the end of the Middle Ages, the adepts of the Free Spirit, who were making widespread progress, must, on the other hand, have contributed to the spreading of the myth (compare the 'Picards' in the Low Countries, whose influence will be found as far away as Bohemia).

One had to wait for the 1300s and 1400s for the myth of the Golden Age to rouse insurgents on its own account. At that time it began to nurture and support the sometimes cruel utopias of popular eschatology, particularly in social groups who thought they had nothing to lose and everything to gain from an uprising.

(A) The English Peasants' Revolt of 1381

The utopia of the Golden Age showed all the violence of which it was capable during the so-called 'artisans' uprising. We have seen that Wat Tyler seems to have been one of the few insurgent leaders in the Middle Ages, if not the only one, to cut something of the figure of a revolutionary leader. This is precisely because he made use of the myth of the egalitarian and communist state.

This myth is particularly apparent in John Ball's pronouncements, which is not to say that the uprising, for the majority of its participants, had a truly egalitarian meaning. In addition to the famous saying ("When Adam delved . . .") reported by a St Albans monk, Thomas Walsingham, Froissart's account seems to confirm the egalitarian character of John Ball's ideas: after a violent attack on the lords, Ball apparently concluded that "things cannot go well in England nor ever shall until all things are in common and there is neither villein nor noble, but all of us are of one condition". It must be said that Wyclif had developed the same ideas in the preceding years, notably in his *De civili dominio* (1374), itself inspired by scholastic writings. These ideas had been familiar to the English since the appearance of a *Dialogue of Dives and Pauper* at the start of the fourteenth century. "All good things of God ought to be in common", Wyclif had written, "Every man ought to be lord of the whole world. But, because of the multitudes of men, this will not happen unless they all hold all things in common: therefore all things ought to be in common." But it was only a theory to the author, a scholarly exercise which ought not to be applied to secular society. Is it not possible that Oxford students took his thesis literally and made themselves its propagandists?

Unlike authors of sermons or Wyclif himself, John Ball proclaimed that the time was ripe for the coming of an egalitarian millennium: it would not just be the Kingdom of Saints, as messianic leaders had been asserting for such a long time, it would really be a second Golden Age. And Ball was readily listened to by members of the lower clergy, who were eager to assume the role of inspired prophets in the town as well as in the country. This is one of the reasons why the 1381 revolt was both a 'Jacquerie' and a London movement. At that time, there were a great many marginals in the English countryside as well as in London, and they were ready-made recruits for the 'prophets'. It was believed that everything was going to be made new, that the social norms and barriers were going to collapse. And certain aspects of the violence can only be explained in the light of millenarianism: for example the burning of the palace of the Savoy and the destruction of all the treasures it contained by people who wanted to take nothing for themselves; the impractical demands among those addressed to the sovereign at Smithfield; or Jack Straw's admission, if he ever made it, that all nobles and clergy (with the exception of certain Mendicants) were to have been exterminated. Without going so far, Wat Tyler, for his part, had ended up elaborating a programme of almost total 'revolution' for society: was he really a revolutionary in the sense that we understand the word, or an insurgent who was completely and utterly steeped in the egalitarianism of the new messianism?

(B) The Taborite uprising (1420–c.1434)

The significance and extent of the Hussite and Taborite movement in Bohemia in the early part of the fifteenth century are well known. In several respects this movement had millenarian and egalitarian characteristics. We know too that criticism of the Church had long been very severe, both because the Church in Bohemia was very rich and especially because the prelates were generally German, not Czech: Czech bitterness against the German minority assured there would be a good deal of support for any movement which was hostile to the Church.

As early as the 1360s, the ascetic, John Milíč, had enjoyed great popularity in Prague; he called on the clergy to live a life of poverty, foretelling at the same time that the coming of Antichrist was imminent. His demand for profound reforms was readily echoed by the Czech population and the demand was renewed when Wyclif's theses became known, namely around 1380. Even more important, about 1400, John Huss took up these bitter condemnations of the Church, and fairly soon his influence passed beyond the Bohemian borders. Huss was primarily a popular preacher who achieved great success through his severe censure of the corruption and worldliness of the clergy. But when he was made head of the University of Prague, he carried great weight among the students and even among important people: he was no longer the spiritual leader of just the humbler classes, but of almost all Czechs. His contentions with the pope and the Council of Constance, and his death in 1415 as a heretic, have been well documented.

The news of his execution turned the unrest felt by the Bohemian people into an openly insurgent movement. The autochthonal nobility placed itself at the head of the uprising. Many clerics were driven out or molested. Under pressure from Pope Martin V, King Wenceslas tried, but in vain, to re-establish order: the advisers appointed by him suffered defenestration and the revolt escalated. It even became a 'national war' and achieved remarkable victories. And the radical wing of the Hussite movement grew stronger because of it (1419).

The members of this radical wing, which was in opposition to the 'Utraquists', were known as the Taborites. Although their 'capital' was in the provinces, at Ústí, many of their adepts were recruited in Prague from amongst artisans, cloth-workers, tailors and brewers, etc., and their adversaries ultimately claimed that the whole Hussite movement had, from the first, been financed by the urban artisan guilds. The lot of the Prague artisans does not seem to have been particularly bad at that time. Yet they had been excluded, as almost everywhere in the West, from municipal administration, which remained in the hands of the often Germanic upper bourgeoisie until the 1419 rising. From July of this year, the guilds took over the administration of the city and expelled those Catholics who had not been converted to Hussitism. Much monastic property was seized, too. The New City thus fell under the control of the artisans, an even more exclusive control than that of the upper bourgeoisie had been.

Outside Prague, the Taborite troops were drawn largely from amongst the marginals, the unemployed and vagabonds, and unqualified and manual workers. It is true that in Prague itself the number of marginals had recently increased considerably, Bohemia having suffered from a massive exodus from rural areas of poor people flocking towards the capital. But artisans, the unemployed and vagabonds were not the only members of the Taborite tactical force; quite large numbers of peasants joined, embittered by nobiliary reactive measures which, since the beginning of the century, had limited their rights. The aspirations of the Taborites were many and confused. The adepts were hostile to feudalism and serfdom mainly because these were thought to be specifically Germanic institutions. One cannot just say that from a religious point of view, and in contrast to the Utraquists, the Taborites were far removed from orthodoxy, since they adopted the essentials of the theses of the Waldensians and Wyclif. One should add that chiliastic leanings, which were already present in Bohemia, became more pronounced with them. A short time previously, Cola di Rienzo had foretold at Prague the imminent arrival of an age of peace, justice and harmony: the paradisiacal order would come tomorrow. John Milíč and the 'reformers' who succeeded him had also lived in a feverish expectation of the Second

Coming of the Saviour. Shortly before 1400, some members of the Free Spirit sect, again a messianic sect, had appeared in Bohemia: in 1418, refugees from Lille and Tournai, the 'Picards', had come and settled in the country. Not content with criticizing the wealth of the clergy, they claimed to be the instruments of the Holy Spirit, possessed of as wide a knowledge of everything as the apostles, or indeed as Christ. They prophesied the imminence of the millennium, of the Third and Last Age, just as the *Homines intelligentiae* of Brussels were doing at the same time.

The way had thus been prepared for an outbreak of millenarianism, and from early in 1420 this was quite acute. As usual, 'prophets' began predicting the Apocalypse and inciting the fanaticism and passions of the lowest social groups. Amongst these leaders there were both unfrocked and regular priests, and they were led by Martin Húska (nicknamed *Loquis* on account of his remarkable eloquence): evil had to be overthrown immediately in order to prepare for the millennium; towns and villages would, like Sodom, be purified by fire between 10 and 14 February 1420, and the wrath of God would fall on those who did not flee to the *mountains*, in other words, the five Taborite bastions.

Following his sudden death during the 1419 troubles in Prague, Wenceslas was succeeded by his brother, Sigismund, who was particularly hostile to the insurgents. We know that in the spring of 1420 he organized an 'international' army to crush the rebellion. But the rebellion's remarkable leader, John Žižka, succeeded in repelling the invaders with great courage and ferocity. This success was very encouraging for the supporters of millenarianism, despite the absence of any disaster in the days before 15 February. Messianic hopes increased both because of military successes and because (paradoxically) the apocalyptic prediction had just failed: new efforts were needed to ensure that the millenium was not delayed again.

The dangers encountered because of the anti-Czech coalition were thus seen as messianic woes prefiguring the end of the wicked and the dawn of a new era. But people were not content with waiting for the miracle which was going to wipe out God's enemies, it was felt that the faithful themselves should undertake the purification of the world: no pity should stay the massacre of the wicked; as soon as the earth was rid of wicked fathers and wicked sons, God would descend from Heaven to meet His saints, the Taborites.

It is impossible to specify what influence may have been exerted by John Ball, the 'Picards', or other adepts of the Free Spirit. In any case, Czech literature – and not only in sermons – was full of explosive ideas well before the birth of the Taborite movement. Three centuries earlier, Cosmas of Prague, the first Bohemian historian, had described the settling of the first men in the country and had depicted their life-style as that of a Golden Age: everything was shared, women as well as wealth! These utopias had been perpetuated from century to century in learned circles. As the Taborites understood it – or at least their extremist wing – the millennium, which was now quite near, was going to be a return to this anarcho-communist order where private property, taxes and rents would be no more. Thus, according to them, it was imperative that "all lords, nobles and knights shall be cut down and exterminated . . . like outlaws". And this applied even more to the merchants – for the rich townsmen were considered more blameworthy than the rural lords; the towns needed to be set fire to and razed to the ground. Once purification was complete and the warrior-Christ had appeared to make war upon Antichrist, the Bohemian Saints would then go forth to conquer the rest of the world: "kings shall serve them, and any nation that will not serve them shall be destroyed; the Sons of God shall tread on the necks of kings and all realms under heaven shall be given unto them."

This plan for a world-wide anarcho-communistic order in reality met with very little success. Early in 1420 the Taborite priests set up communal chests in order that thousands of peasants and artisans could put the proceeds from the sale of their belongings into them. Some fanatics even went as far as burning their homes. Then these men who had renounced all private ownership joined the Taborite army, where they led a community life somewhat similar to that of the *plebs pauperum* of the crusades. The main egalitarian community was established near Ústí, on a promontory where priests had already been taking refuge since 1419; the river flowing at the foot of the promontory was named Jordan and the promontory where a small town was built was called Tabor – hence the name given to the uprising as a whole and its devotees.

The communistic experiment failed. Because of their belief in the myth of the Golden Age, according to which one could live without working, the Taborites gave up cultivating the land. Once the money in the chests had gone, the communist groups had to start making raids in order to live; the victims were peasants who had not joined the cause or who had simply stayed at home. And yet, in the beginning, there had been almost universal enthusiasm among the Czech peasantry since, in the first flush of revolutionary euphoria, the Taborites had proclaimed, in the spring of 1420, the abolition of all feudal bonds, dues and services. But, from October 1420, after the harvest in fact, the appalling economic situation, which had come about because of the disturbances and because fanatical peasants had abandoned their lands, forced the Taborite leaders to levy taxes in the zones which they controlled on those peasants who had stayed where they were. And these taxes soon became so heavy that the villagers found themselves worse off than they had been under their lords. This situation resulted in the beginnings of a split amongst the Taborites. Some took a more moderate attitude; they were sympathetic to the difficulties of the peasants caught as they were between the Taborite army and the opposing forces. At the end of all this, the Bohemian peasantry was going to find itself more impoverished than ever and so weak that the nobility would be able to exploit it as never before.

The anarcho-communistic experiment soon had to be abandoned in the Taborite communities themselves. The millenarians were devoid of any practical common sense and the soldiers were engaged in a very difficult war. At their head was John Žižka, a minor noble who established a firm hierarchy and entrusted all posts of responsibility to other members of the lower nobility experienced in arms (their presence reminds us that all the social strata took part in the rebellion). The most fanatical believers in the return to the Golden Age ended up seeming a danger to the military, who were exasperated by their laziness and illusions, and even more by the preaching of Húska and the agitating of the Pikarti (the 'Picards') whom Žižka had expelled from Tabor and about fifty of whom he had burned as heretics. Those who escaped came to be known as the Bohemian Adamites; they lived in a state of absolute community under the leadership of a former priest, Peter Kániš, until they were hunted down and exterminated by Žižka on 21 October 1421. Thus the millenarian and communist movement had gradually become restricted to the most extreme wing of the Taborites and had ended up being harassed by the rest, who rejected the communism if not the millenarianism.

We know that, in 1422, the Taborite movement in Prague itself was finished. However, the Taborites remained powerful in the country: it was not until 1434 that their army was defeated at Lipany by the Utraquists, and Tabor did not fall until 1452. In the meantime, the millenarian propaganda of the moderate Taborites had spread beyond the Bohemian borders and sympathizers were found in Germany, France and even Spain. But it was only in Germany, which was, of course, nearer, that they went as far as rioting, for example at Mainz, Weimar and Constance. It is not certain that peasant movements in Burgundy and Lyons were influenced by the Taborites, as the clergy believed.

A chiliastic undercurrent persisted in Bohemia and southern Germany, keeping alive the idea of a return to the Golden Age in the popular imagination. In Bavaria, notably, Beghards and shepherds would periodically appear as 'prophets'. Eschatological exaltation is a legacy which the Middle Ages bequeathed to the early modern period.

CHAPTER 2

Rebellion and social mobility

Unlike millenarian movements in which, although the marginals have a prominent part, very different strata are generally represented, the rebellions with which we are now going to deal have, when they begin, members of only one or two strata taking part, although they might later succeed in rousing other social categories.

These movements are started either by a new social group which wishes to belong to the elites, or by elites who are not satisfied with their lot in comparison with some other elites. In both cases the malcontents consider, rightly or wrongly, that the circulation of elites is blocked or insufficient, and that they have not been given the position they deserve. But in the first category, there is a new and active social group, which can be large or small and which is due to the acceleration of social mobility, whilst in the second, there is a serious division at the heart of the elites and not only because as a whole they lack homogeneity. At such a time social mobility seems to be checked. Some other social group may profit from this division.

In general, the term 'revolt', as defined above, pp. 20–25, is not really suitable here. There is no despair, especially in the first category, and fairly often the malcontents are not motivated just by conservatism. But the word 'revolution' is not suitable either: the malcontents do not call society as a whole into question. Since it is vaguer than 'revolt' we thus prefer to use the term 'rebellion'.

Rebellion and the birth of the bourgeoisie

We are all aware of how Pirenne's theses on the origin of the first bourgeois and the bourgeoisie, after being too highly praised, have now been too greatly discredited. If it is not generally true that the first burghers were, as he believed, nomadic folk from distant places, if there were peasants and even nobles from the neighbouring region amongst them, it is none the less true that, in the minds of the nobles and the clergy, these new groups had scarcely any place in the feudal system. For their part, the burghers complained of being ignored by the system, which seemed unable to offer any solution to their problems, which were more particularly of a commercial nature. In short, the bourgeois wanted to free themselves from various fetters and they wanted to be recognized as a new elite by the ruling elites, who would thus make room at their side for a dominant elite (since they practised the dominant urban occupation, namely trade, sometimes involving the *artisanat*, sometimes not). The candidates for the rank of dominant elite wanted to have their say in the solving of urban economic problems. However, they also wanted to participate in the administration of the developing towns, whether new or old. Thus they also wanted to become a ruling elite. But did they want to act alongside or in place of the old urban directive elites?

Did these nascent elites, who of course wanted to be recognized as elites, obtain their privileges through bargaining, blackmail or violence? To what extent was the rise of the new elites due to, or accompanied by, violence and rebellion? For example, was the commune ("a new and loathsome word") born mainly of violence?

Our view is distorted because contemporary writers preferred to leave us an account of those 'freedoms' which were born of violence, no doubt because any others did not provide matter for sensational elaboration.

Pirenne proved very clearly that one of the stimuli behind urban and bourgeois emancipation was the need for peace and security, a need which grew stronger in almost all the social strata throughout the eleventh century. Indeed this is why violence is not a constant feature in the history of the nascent bourgeoisie. We shall not follow Augustin Thierry, who was still too close to the Revolution and the view that it was the outcome of the communal movement. He was also reacting against ideas fashionable under Louis XVIII (compare the preamble to the 1814 Charter which refers to the communes' apparently owing "their emancipation to Louis the Fat"), when, for example, he asserted that "the commune, throughout its entire development, was scarcely ever achieved except by open force". For him, it was "the terrible awakening of the spirit of democracy at a time of order and voluntary obedience". A. Luchaire and Ch. Petit-Dutaillis have corrected the more exaggerated aspects of this viewpoint: although it is deep-rooted, the idea that the 'commune' has a revolutionary (compare the use of this word in 1871) echo is incorrect. The point of departure for their critique lies in a long under-estimated fact: this desire for *peace* which often induced lords to authorize the formation of the communal bond and to grant franchises. It is absurd to imagine an entire seignorial world which was incapable of seeing beyond immediate benefits, which ignored the general interest, and was unable to understand that security was, in the long term, going to bring the lords important benefits in the town and in the country. As many lords were aware, seignorial and bourgeois interests were not opposed, and the future was to show that, in general, relations between nobles and burghers were good.

The situation has been falsified because of the insistence with which one has cited the *co-juratio* of one commune which was founded in violence – and what violence! – and then suppressed by violence before being re-established by mutual accord, namely the commune of Laon. A very detailed account of this has been left us by an eyewitness, one Guibert, the abbot of Nogent-sous-Coucy. He was a malicious witness, an avowed opponent of the communal movement, but his account was taken up by Augustin Thierry.

One also has to be wary of invective from the clerical chroniclers and preachers, since in those days the clergy seems to have been insensible to economic necessities. Petit-Dutaillis has even gone as far as to lament "the poverty of their grievances, the emptiness of their thoughts and the insincerity of their judgements" . . .. But not all the clerics were as blind. The excesses committed in a few rare towns were of minor importance compared with the benefits of *friendship*: if one could compile statistics, one would see that, in the vast majority of towns, normal relations were the rule between the clergy and the bourgeois. Let us not confuse quarrels and conflicts where there were no disturbances with riots! Even prelates formed alliances with the burghers, as in 1089 at Le Mans, where they wanted to oppose some local tyrant engaged in brigandage and whom they eventually besieged in his château. And without moving far from Laon, one can quote as illustrations of alliances between the clergy and townsmen, Noyon, Ham, Beauvais and Amiens. For their part, princes and kings realized, like certain prelates, that "the formation of the communal bond (or the concession of simple franchises) was a means of defence against the covetousness and brutality of minor feudalism": this was so in Picardy itself. Then, as order returned to France, another preoccupation filled the minds of the powerful and the monarchy: they wanted to strengthen the royal or princely power and to extract from the communes the same benefits and obedience as they would from a vassal.

Before 1200, union between royalty and bourgeoisie was a fact in royal France, and it was the same in the great fiefs: except perhaps in the very long term, the bourgeoisie was not the death-knell of the 'feudal system'. Marxists would have done better to draw conclusions from a fact which they themselves brought clearly to light: the insertion of bourgeois collectivities into the feudal framework.

For the commune gradually became a *seigneurie collective*. Philip Augustus understood better than anyone how much the communal association, in which the members bound themselves together by oath, could support him against his adversaries, especially against the Plantagenets. It was really this gifted ruler who established the alliance between the Capetians and the bourgeois of the towns, whether they were communes or not. From the communes within his demesne and from those which were outside, but which had prudently asked the king for confirmation of their franchises and privileges, he exacted the same services, mainly of a military nature, as from his vassals. Thus almost everywhere in the kingdom bourgeois collective seigniories were born. And the mayor was represented on the seal of many communes as a warrior ... as a knight, since he commanded the militia. And we know that the communal militias marched on Bouvines in 1214: it is true that they arrived after the battle, but this did not indicate any the less their loyalty to the king, who was being dangerously pressed by the allies of John Lackland. One century later, the Flemish militias put the French chivalry to flight, demonstrating the valour of the bourgeois warriors and the military importance of the towns. In any case, the towns showed themselves to be more loyal to their natural lord than some nobles. But there was also a financial aspect in all this: the towns were subject to the taxes laid down by feudal custom. These were an excellent source of revenue for the king, duke or count, who would often appeal to the purse of their urban 'vassals' for help. We do not have to go into the details of the process, but it is necessary to recall the general and lasting accord which grew up quite early on between the feudal or royal directors and the burghers – in other words, between the different elites.

Pirenne spoke of the "urban democracies", as did Augustin Thierry – wrongly. The *consensus* which existed in the beginning did not last and the primitive bourgeoisie itself did not form just one stratum. Very soon there were at least two groups, the elite and the *commonalty*, whose interests, once the franchises or commune had been won, diverged. The leaders of the protest movement were not always rich burghers, as the case of Laon shows. But when the town became 'major', especially when the right of self-government was conceded, an oligarchy soon broke away from the majority of the bourgeois, and strove to secure important posts. Worse still, the dominant families, who were also directive in the case of the commune, often took great liberties in matters of finance, making sure of fat profits for themselves while forcing the commonalty to bear almost the entire brunt of taxation. Why did St Louis, who so respected the rights of others, place under protection those towns which were all, in future, to be labelled 'good towns'? It was because he was deeply shocked by the fiscal inequality between townsmen and by the dishonesty of some, and the injustice of most, 'patrician' oligarchies. True, it was a good pretext for getting money for the monarchy, but it was not just a pretext. If the towns complained of the severity of the burdens imposed by the king, it was partly to conceal the resentment felt by the rich burghers at being placed under the surveillance of royal agents who had the common good more at heart than they did. One can see the advantages for the non-elite of having a strong royal power, as was the case in France and even more so in England. On the other hand, in regions where the prince was weak or in those – admittedly rare – where the towns carried exceptional weight (mainly in Flanders), the commonalty continued to be exploited financially and corrupt practices continued to prosper.

The bourgeois elite – the financiers and important textile merchants in particular – which was especially powerful, of course, in the great centres, was later going to delay or prevent the political and social emancipation of the strata which constituted the commonalty. But for a long time the conflicts which broke out in different towns in France and its neighbouring territories, were not, properly speaking, conflicts between the bourgeois elite, linked henceforth with older elites, and the commonalty. Thus in the case of Liège, F. Vercauteren has ably shown that even in the thirteenth century, conflicts were born of oppositions between prince, clergy, *échevinage* and patriciate: "The popular masses, who had real power from this period onwards, were solicited by one or the other of the opponents to take its side in the conflict." In this case, the intrusion of the commonalty was thus only that of a tactical force. This was often to be the role of the commonalty for a long time to come.

Outside France and England, the actual forming of the bourgeois elites, and their characteristics too, were not the same everywhere, particularly on the other side of the Alps. "The towns of the *regnum Italiae* – wrote the late Y. Renouard – contain, because of their history and their continuity, a population of major and minor landowners, the land being either inside or outside the towns." The initial ruling group was made up of nobles, to whom became added merchants and artisans, themselves also landowners. These nobles, who were not of the highest birth, were most often the bishop's vassals. As for the upper nobility, which lived in the country, it was not hostile to the development of the towns: it was the "modifying of the feudal world", for example its weakening, which forced the ground-landlords and the usufructuaries of church lands living in the towns "to seek an autonomous organization for urban life".

In Italy, "the merchants did not play a major part in the formation of the communes, which often appeared in order to palliate the temporary inadequacy of the lawful power, and sometimes received help from the emperor, as in Verona, Genoa and Turin" (Renouard). Another fundamental difference from what happened north of the Alps was that "the commune was not a sworn association of equals . . ., but a simple coming together of individuals for the government of the town, in accordance with Roman tradition". Thus, the commune was created by nobles, or with their help, and the towns became part of feudalism without destroying it: in some respects, one arrives at conclusions similar to those valid for northern Europe. But in Italy the commune was more often than in France formed to oppose the bishop, since he was frequently the trustee of the count's dues and many noble vassals were dependent on him: it was opposition to the bishop which gave the Italian communes, in many cases, self-awareness, and not membership of a merchant group as in the north.

The Italian cities achieved almost complete autonomy from the eleventh century, thus in more instances and at an earlier date than was the case in France (at least northern France, for the developments in the south were similar in some respects to those which took place in Italy, because, for example, of the presence of many nobles). The autonomous commune then evolved according to a plan in which Renouard has distinguished four stages. At first, the commune was directed by consuls and was aristocratic in character: the elite was composed mainly of nobles who monopolized power. Then, in a second stage, the aristocracy split up into factions which tore the town apart: the trading milieu and the *artisanat* took advantage of this to demand the setting up of a power of arbitration, which was entrusted to a podestà. In the third stage, the mass of the *populus* (= commonalty + powerful burghers) organized itself into craft-guilds and also formed armed groups for each quarter (*pedites*); it presented the nobles with its own alternative organization to the aristocratic commune. In fact, it was the dominant elite, the *popolo grasso*, the bourgeois of the wealthiest guilds, who were in future to control the town to the resentment of the *popolo minuto* (= commonalty?) which, in its turn, was also gradually becoming organized. It was at this stage that the Italian commune bore the greatest resemblance to northern European cities. But, the fourth and last stage moved away from this and we are reminded that the Italian commune was often a *city-state*: supported by the *popolo minuto*, a noble or a burgher would set up the régime of the *signoria*, which soon became hereditary and authoritarian and put an end to urban freedom. This happened frequently at the end of the Middle Ages.

Renouard stressed one of the dominant characteristics of the evolution of the Italian towns, namely "the importance of family, social, professional or political groups" to the detriment of the notion of the individual. Certainly it was not just in Italy that society organized itself "in dynamic groupings resulting from physical bonds forged by blood, geographical proximity and common interests". But these bonds did play a much more active role in the Italian towns than elsewhere. From the eleventh century, noble families had a residence in the city; they were even obliged to live there in the following century. Each *casato* lived in a fortified palace and the families which sprang from it settled nearby: "the *consorteria* thus owned a complete block of property, above which it erected high towers for keeping watch, for attack and defence" (for example at Bologna, Lucca, San Giminiano). In short, the *consorteria* was a group of knights, a 'tower society'. One can see the consequences during troubled times. For its part, the *popolo* followed the example of the nobles: groups of families joined together around the most powerful family, at first simply because they all lived near each other: these were the "military societies of the gate or quarter", who united under the banner of their quarter and obeyed a captain or gonfalonier. It goes without saying that, here as elsewhere, the craft-guilds were in existence. In addition, one remembers the commercial societies which brought together members of important families, whether noble or bourgeois: groups of opposing interests were formed and thus groups of opposing societies. And the conflict between the Guelphs and the Ghibellines further complicated matters.

But the different conflicts did not take place between individuals. Because of the strength of the feeling of belonging, the options of each individual were governed by loyalty to the *consorteria* or *parte*, to the large group or family, before loyalty to the town itself (as Dante saw so well in his *Inferno*). Consequently, when there are riots and rebellions, it will always be these group solidarities, the alliances between the groups or the hatred which separates them, which will best throw light on the history of urban rebellions in Italy. This history is complicated by the interactions between these groups which, until the end of the Middle Ages, carry much more weight than the economic motivation of any individual. Thus nothing is further from the Marxist panorama than, for example, medieval Florence.

Rebellion and the extension or division of the elites

Although the people cannot rise up as a whole against the elites, except within the framework of very small political units, the division of the elites, especially directive elites, has been the cause of numerous rebellions throughout the centuries. This is particularly true if the additional problem exists of a circulation of elites which causes extreme dissatisfaction to certain social groups, when individuals wish to climb up in the hierarchy and join one of the elites.

For the sake of simplification, we shall look at the two main aspects which can be seen in the Middle Ages, the case of people belonging to the 'commonalty' who want to become part of an elite and that of an elite which wishes to share the prerogatives peculiar to another elite.

(A) Attempts of guildsmen to accede to the rank of elite

This is the problem raised by M. Mollat and Ph. Wolff when they described the constitution of a "sort of middle class", the undertakings of the "middle ranks" against the "rich", thus against the controlling oligarchy in the towns. We have already given our reasons for rejecting the term 'class'. And one could question the adjective 'middle', which is convenient but vague. Henri Mougin has judiciously written that it is a "dangerous illusion to believe that the middle classes are automatically fixed when the extremes are". The extremes here are the oligarchy and the lower strata of the *commonalty*. Fr. Simiand was able to speak of middle classes for the capitalist period, but can one really do so for the preceding period?

It is true that the upper strata of the common people tried, both successfully and unsuccessfully, to realize their own strength. But it was in order to form themselves into an elite, a new elite which would be in opposition to the dominant elite (or directive as well) of the *patriciate*. Around 1280 some guildsmen, causing, on occasions, quite a disturbance, "knocked on the doors of the *échevinages* and consulates; and some of them managed to infiltrate these", thanks to the support of humble people who served them as a tactical force.

In this connection, Pirenne spoke of a "revolution of guilds", which developed rapidly from the first half of the fourteenth century in the Low Countries, almost everywhere in France, in Italy, Mediterranean Spain and the Rhineland. The movement did not, however, develop with the same speed everywhere: it began early in Flanders, but won for its partisans access to the municipal government of certain towns in the Empire in the second half of the fourteenth century only; in some places this happened later. We shall reject the term 'revolution' but shall not forget how much we are indebted to Pirenne for his pioneer work on this problem. In any case he himself found his formula too narrow, since sometimes, as in maritime Flanders, well-to-do peasants also tried to accede to an elite.

In the Low Countries, the guildsmen's opportunity came from the "identifying of their lot with a national cause" at a time when they believed they had reached the limits of tolerance. Disturbances had already broken out here and there around 1280, but they had been suppressed. On the other hand, around 1300, circumstances were generally more favourable for political reasons. However, here as elsewhere, the occupying elite resisted, and not unsuccessfully, since there was almost as much conflict between the guilds as there was between them and the 'patriciate': any 'class consciousness' is hardly noticeable.

Through Espinas we are familiar with the history of Douai. There was a confrontation between patricians and people of the commonalty in a church there in September 1296. And for ten years thereafter the old directive elite and the leaders of the opposition enjoyed power in turns, while the different repressions also alternated, and at the same time the royal officers tried to take control of the town. Several riots broke out in 1304–5; they had been organized by clerics and also by some butchers, whose attempts to accede to the rank of a new elite were now in evidence. One fact in Flanders is significant: Count Guy de Dampierre supported the artisans – the *Clauwaerts* – against the rich burghers who were followers of Philip the Fair – the *Leliaerts* – and it was not long before he became a demagogue. The warring count and king then tried to outdo each other. Guy gave back to Douai and Bruges the freedoms which they had lost after the 1280 movements, and he condemned the corrupt practices of the ruling and dominant elite of Ghent. The king, for his part, went as far as to concede to the guildsmen half the echevin posts in Ghent; but his maladroit representatives alienated the cloth-workers by supporting the patricians, then by brutally repressing trouble stemming from the fiscal demands of the monarchy. We know what followed, particularly the Bruges insurrection under the leadership of Peter de Coninck who, with the count, united the guildsmen against the royal troops and the *Leliaerts.* There was a conflict on two fronts: against Philip the Fair and against the old bourgeois elite; they were defeated in 1302 in the Battle of the Golden Spurs. Should one necessarily see a "revolutionary triumph" in this battle? It was more a prefiguration of the French defeats in the Hundred Years War, which were due to incompetent cavalry charges made against foot-soldiers, in this case the urban infantrymen. In any event, for at least some years, the old patrician elite had to give way in most of the Flemish *échevinages* to representatives of the highest stratum of the commonalty, thus raised to the rank of a new elite. Probably through contagiousness, riots broke out in neighbouring principalities (Brabant, Liège and so on): as early as 1302 in Brussels, and in 1312 in Liège, there was pillaging and some killing. But, at least in Brabant, this brought no success as far as the guilds were concerned.

The victory of the Flemish craft-guilds, or to be more exact, of the most powerful ones, could not last. This was, perhaps, not so much because of the schemings of the old elite, which had not given up its desire for revenge, as because of a lack of agreement between the wealthier artisans: the feeling of a common interest between all the guilds suffered as a result of the rivalry which existed between them (fullers against weavers, urban textile workers against rural artisans and so on). Each guild, jealous of its privileges, was already becoming crystallized, incapable of adapting to a new situation, and desirous of limiting the number of its members. High-ranking artisans already wanted to reserve places in the *échevinat* and the best positions in the guild for their own families. In short, this elite, having succeeded in its ends, immediately wished to block any future circulation of elites and prevent all social promotion for anyone else. The history of Ghent, which H. Van Werveke has set out so clearly, shows the alliance between the fullers – always on bad terms with the weavers – and the rich *poorters* against the weavers. This lasted from 1319 to 1337. We know that in James van Artevelde's time there was a mortal confrontation between fullers and weavers in 1345: James was to be assassinated some two months later during a riot organized, this time, by the weavers. But the fullers enjoyed their revenge on 13 January 1349: having already been defeated a short time previously at Bruges and at Ypres, the weavers were massacred at Ghent; according to Gilles le Muisi, there were six thousand victims. Although the victors, the fullers were not, however, to accede to the rank of the elite as was their ambition: in 1350, those weavers who had survived the massacre, in turn massacred them, which meant the end of their influence for a long time to come. In short, as opposition to the elites formed by the merchant drapers, only the influential and respected craft-guilds, like that of the weavers, had some chance of taking part in the government of the towns. What one sees here is a second stage, a second bourgeois elite wanting a place alongside the patrician elite on account of both its economic domination and its management of *échevinal* affairs. Once installed, the second elite blocked competition from other guilds. Thus, from 1369 in Ghent, there were in the urban tribunal three seats for the *poorters*, five for the weavers and only five for all the other guilds, who were certain to be almost always in the minority.

In the Empire, urban troubles would seem to exemplify a division of elites, but one which favoured the accession of new elites. The political parcelling-up of the country had repercussions which meant that the evolution varied considerably from one town to the next. One can more or less distinguish three waves of guild rebellions: the first was around 1300; the second, which won the guilds access to the town's affairs, temporarily or otherwise, dates from 1327; and the third was in the middle of the fourteenth century, a period when disorders became widespread. In some towns, such as Zurich or Strasbourg, the urban 'patriciate' was not entirely made up of burghers: one found side by side nobles and commoners who envied and opposed each other. Now these nobles were fairly numerous, and in Strasbourg they constituted the great majority of the magistracy (Ph. Dollinger). Thus the rich burghers formed an alliance with the craft-guilds there in 1332, following an affray. Of course, the artisans were used only as a tactical force, a means of pressure which finally allowed the important burghers to dominate Strasbourg. In a fatal reversal of this alliance, during the 1349 pogroms, the guilds sided with the nobility. A riot gave power back to the nobles but they allowed the artisans only a minimal share of it . . . and this situation was to last until 1789!

In Zurich, on the other hand, the nobles did not dominate the upper bourgeoisie. Thus the 1356 rebellion was an artisan movement against both nobles and burghers at the same time. The disturbances, which were protracted and weakened the economic strength of the town, brought only illusory satisfaction to the artisans. But Zurich, like Strasbourg, is something of an exception: in most other imperial towns, the guilds were not so hostile to the old elites in power; they were content to have just some part in the urban administration. In these towns disturbances and expulsions were neither very serious nor really frequent.

On the whole, one can distinguish three groups among the towns of the Empire. The first comprised the towns of the south-west which apparently had, according to H. Planitz, a 'democratic' aspect. The craft-guilds seem to have won a victory, complete in Magdeburg and Speyer and elsewhere, and somewhat moderated (the rich bourgeois keeping an important weighting in the urban council) in Strasbourg, Fribourg, Basel and Worms; victory had to wait until 1396 in Cologne, where the patrician elite was exceptionally coherent. A new elite was thus able to penetrate these Swiss, Alsatian and Swabian regions. The second group, short-lived, comprised a few towns such as Constance, Haguenau and especially Vienna where guilds and old elite found themselves on an equal footing in the council. However, this was such a fragile situation that, sooner or later, one of the parties was bound to gain the upper hand. Finally, the third group was that of the powerful northern Hanse towns: here, around 1400, unlike what happened in many other Germanic towns, the rich merchants, despite some violence and some very fleeting concessions to the guilds, succeeded in preventing the rise of a new directive elite (see below, p. 158).

The Italian cities present a somewhat different aspect. The rich commercial bourgeoisie – the *popolo grasso* – had only been able to restrain and gradually erode the powers of the old aristocracy of the *magnati*, which had long been powerful in many cities, with the co-operation of the *popolo minuto*, which was made up of many artisans, some of whom were quite wealthy, indeed very wealthy. We know that subsequently there was frequent discord between the two groups of *popolani*, the *grassi* imposing a harsh economic domination on the other inhabitants, whom they sometimes regarded with contempt, and the *minuti* demanding, without much success, some participation in the city's administration. Each time the external situation was disturbed, the merchant oligarchy, which was at once directive and dominant, had to face demands and sometimes disturbances. This was so from around 1300 onwards.

Venice is an example of a city where the splitting-up of the elite in power instigated popular movements which were , however, destined to fail. Since 1297, the government had been exclusively in the hands of the oligarchy; as the people's assembly had lost its powers and the Great Council had "closed itself" to newcomers, some two hundred families had a monopoly of all the seats. And the signoria and the doge were only the executive agents of the members of the elite. Now in 1299, a conspiracy and a 'popular' movement against the doge failed. Why? It is curiously significant that the entire population, although excluded from public affairs, supported the oligarchy: the conspirators were in no way expressing the wishes of the 'people', they had been manipulated by powerful families who, despite their wealth, were none the less excluded from the Great Council. In short, some patricians belonged only to the dominant elite and were excluded from the political elite. Later on, other conspiracies were likewise only to set opposing patrician factions against each other: one of these conspiracies, in the 1340s, had a bloody outcome, but it was an excellent illustration of the fear the rich merchants had of seeing an alliance formed between the doge and the artisans.

It was not only in Venice that powerful merchants tried to bar the entry of newcomers and wealthy artisans and prevent their becoming a new elite. Occasionally, however, as in Siena, they had given way, from 1280, to the wealthiest artisans, so that the lower strata, manipulated by the nobles, the heads of the minor arts or even rival merchants, were seen only as an insignificant mass whose interests were defended by no one. In 1315, there was fighting in the streets in an attempt to get the better of the Salimbeni, rivals of the Tolomei. Three years later, the signoria was invaded: this time the movement was directed against the rich artisans who formed the new elite. In Genoa, on the other hand, at the end of the thirteenth century and in the early 1300s, the disturbances were more anti-nobiliary in character, and they allowed the rise of a new ruling elite, in this case formed of important burghers. We are familiar with the frailty of the Genoese political system, which resulted from the rivalry between the Guelphs and the Ghibellines. Thus it was *popolani*, but especially members of the powerful merchant aristocracy, who arbitrated in the quarrels between the Doria and the Spinola, Ghibelline nobles, and the Grimaldi and the Fieschi, Guelph nobles. In 1339, a riot by sailors and silk-workers expelled all the Guelph nobles and appointed a Ghibelline, Simone Boccanegra, as lord for life. Thus the old noble elite, by being divided, had allowed both a new elite to come to power and the creation of the first personal lordship in Italian history; soon many more examples of this phenomenon were to be found, often following a period of unrest, and they generally had the support of the lower strata.

The case of Florence is also remarkably well-known. In theory, the rich burghers and influential artisans won their cause there earlier than elsewhere. In 1284, a council of the commune had been organized where the artisans had a say along with the nobles, the *magnati* and the *popolani* (in effect, only the rich bourgeois): in reality, the upper bourgeoisie regarded the 'minor' artisans only as an occasional means of support. What has been called the regime of the *secondo popolo* then began. Less than ten years later, the nobles were removed and, following a riot, they were to be in future second-class citizens. Giano della Bella, a nobleman, had roused the guildsmen and declared his wish to give some standing even to the minor artisans. But he was deserted by some of his followers and had to go into exile: he was reproached, as happens frequently in such cases, with not having kept his promises.

The history of Florence brings out clearly the difference between the word '*popolo*' and our term 'people'. Sometimes *popolo* indicates only the upper stratum of the city population; thus the *popolo grasso* which was formed by the higher business bourgeoisie, the new ruling or political elite from 1284. Sometimes *popolo* is taken in its widest meaning, but it does not include all the people, since anyone who had not joined a guild (for example, a certain number of workers) and anyone practising a trade which had not formed a guild, was excluded. In its widest sense, the Florentine *popolo* comprises the whole of the 'arts' (= organized guilds), it being understood that the rights of the journeymen (= *sottoposti*) carried little weight compared to those of the masters of the twelve principle 'arts'. These 'arts', the basis of Florentine political structures since 1284, were divided into groups. The *popolo grasso* was made up of seven greater 'arts', among them the Arte di Calimala for wool, the Arte della Seta for silk, and the 'arts' of the drapers and money-changers. The *grassi*, who had just gained power in 1284 and the following years, were exceedingly wealthy men who had succeeded in combining greatness with their wealth. Amongst these new families, no longer merely dominant but ruling as well, were the Peruzzi, Acciaiuoli, Alberti, Albizzi, Strozzi, Pitti and Medici, this last family reaching its greatest heights in the following centuries. Beneath the seven greater 'arts' there were five *intermediate 'arts'*, including those of the retail cloth-dealers, the linen-manufacturers, the silk-workers and also the butchers: the masters were comfortably-off or even fairly rich men who, in the face of the exclusive government of the *popolo grasso*, disposed of a militia and a council (just as in the greater 'arts') within each intermediate 'art' created after the 1250 uprising. Sooner or later, the intermediate 'arts' were to claim a place in the government and they were to be strong enough to create pressure and accede, in their turn, to the rank of ruling elite. Finally, there were the nine *minor 'arts'*, formed from 1288–9 and comprising the wine-merchants, salt-merchants, oil- and cheese-merchants, the bakers and tanners and the like. Although in theory future government was in the hands of all the 'arts', in practice the *grassi* had already taken and reserved all the important posts: through a harsh but effective piece of legislation they were to prevent the masters of other 'arts' from raising themselves to the rank of ruling elite for a long time (the artisans were closely watched under the pretext that the quality of their products had to be carefully supervised).

The great Florentine merchants thus blocked the rise of new elites. But they often joined with the masters of other 'arts' in order to obstruct social promotion at a lower level by blocking any attempts by the *sottoposti* to gain access to the consulates (the consuls being the heads of the 'arts'). In the long term this was all the more dangerous as the city was torn between the two Guelph factions, the Whites and the Blacks. The latter were defeated in 1304 and Dante was exiled. Despite this success, the elite in power was particularly fearful of an alliance between the followers of the Blacks and the guildsmen who were excluded from the government. But only the intermediate 'arts' were going to gain some ground. For the *grassi* were able to withstand the storm during the lordship of Walter of Brienne (1342–3), who had been called upon to arbitrate between the factions and who saw himself, apparently at least, as a man of the minor 'arts': there was a riot, involving principally dyers and carders, during which dozens of patrician palaces were set on fire before it was crushed.

If we look back to a time shortly before the Black Death of 1348–1350, we see that although the upper stratum of the bourgeoisie had had some successes against the nobles in places where the nobles were a danger or a barrier to them (thus mainly in Italy), on the other hand this dominant and ruling elite had only rarely made way, alongside or beneath it, for a second ruling elite; this second elite would likewise be bourgeois and well-to-do or even rich and would be recruited from amongst those members of the strata immediately below the upper stratum who already constituted, but only to a certain extent, a dominant elite. A new combination of circumstances was subsequently to modify this state of things, this blocking of the circulation of elites and of social promotion. But it was not to happen everywhere nor to be long-lasting.

(B) Moves by one elite against the political elite

The seizure of political power from the nobles in the cities by the Italian *grassi* was an early example of troubles caused by the division of elites. In the pages which follow we shall leave the *city-states* for wider political fields, the great Western kingdoms. But due to lack of space, we shall be able to note only some of the more famous French examples.

Sometimes the picture painted of Etienne Marcel is hardly flattering: he is depicted as too cunning an orator, a demagogue manipulating the people rather too much, ending up as a traitor, since his collusion with Charles the Bad was, indirectly, a collusion with the English invaders. Thus he was a traitor to his country and, even worse, to his king. Sometimes, and this was fashionable amongst historians who followed the 1789 ideology, the provost of the merchants was put on a pedestal; he was seen as the fierce opponent of absolute monarchy (which, however, did not yet exist in the fourteenth century . . .) and of spendthrift officers, and as the defender of the bourgeoisie in the face of the overbearing nobility which wallowed in its privileges. Neither of these contradictory portraits is completely true.

What is certain is that the provost of the merchants in no way foreshadowed the 1789 Revolution. In many respects he was just a simple insurgent, since he looked more towards the past. His criticisms of all the underhand dealings which were prevalent at the time and which had been made worse by the military disasters, his desire to have some control over the monarchy, especially in matters of finance, and his demand that the consent of the Estates be obtained for the levying of taxes, were certainly, in theory, very justified, and they do have a 'modern' ring. But if France was not the object of any serious external threat in 1789, the same was not true after Poitiers! We must not forget that, if monarchical power in France was being almost constantly strengthened, this was precisely because – Mousnier has insisted on this with regard to the seventeenth century – France was for centuries very frequently under threat. This was particularly true in 1355–1358 when, far from being 'tyrannical', the royal power was too weak and ill-obeyed. Strengthening the power of the towns against it, wanting to unite the towns into a league, as Etienne Marcel desired, were similar kinds of utopias to those dreamed of by the Girondists when the Revolution was threatened with a coalition – a justification rather than a pretext for the Jacobin policy of a 'strong' power.

Who were Etienne Marcel's first supporters? Sincere malcontents or ambitious men ('ambitious' does not necessarily have any pejorative connotations here)? There is no need to emphasize how manifold were the subjects for justified discontent: the bad economic situation, the weight of fiscal dues, the various consequences of the military defeats and capture of John the Good. At the beginning of 1357 the provost and the bishop of Laon, Robert le Coq, wielded considerable influence in the Estates General, which were calling for the dismissal of those royal advisers who came from families of high-ranking notables and who were accused of all sorts of misdeeds. This was characteristic: through the medium of the man who was for a time its spokesman, the wealthy Parisian merchant bourgeoisie clearly intimated that it no longer wished to be the ruling elite just of Paris and its economy, but that it wished to supplant the political elite which controlled the state at that time, in other words the elite of office-holding notables. And the great ordinance of 3 March 1357, together with measures for the control of the monarchical finances, was like a call to revolt. Did it not proclaim that, if the legitimate authority should lapse, the French had the right to "assemble . . . in order to put up a stand against (it)", and even to use force to counter the authorities? Other measures were aimed at winning over the sympathies of the guildsmen (whom the rich merchants did not treat any better here than elsewhere) and even of the marginals to the provost of the merchants who, through his office, had supreme control over all the commerce of the capital, *as well as* over the *artisanat*: measures were decreed for the protection of the *povres gens*. Moreover, since 19 and 20 January, Marcel, in protest against another change in the currency (a customary but always unpopular expedient of governments in need), had already organized a general strike of guildsmen and had not been afraid to "send an order through the entire city for everyone to be armed".

We know that on 28 February 1358, in order to intimidate the dauphin, the provost set 3,000 artisans to attack the royal dwelling; two marshals were assassinated and Charles was forced to don the two colours of Paris. Should one see in this humiliation of the royal power and this 'organized' riot the prefiguration of 20 June 1792? In no way, for most of these rioters were prompted by 'reactionary' feelings. They wanted to go back – as if one could go back in time . . . – to the institutions and government of St Louis, who had remained so popular that the collective mentality still felt an incredible nostalgia for his reign. But the desire for a return to the old ways did not exist only in the ranks of the insurgent artisans and marginals: Marcel won the co-operation of nobles who did not belong to the *notables* and who were thus hostile to the political elite which held power. These nobles wanted to resume the action formerly undertaken by their fathers after the death of Philip the Fair, and to take charge of the king's council so as seriously to limit the sovereign's power. But, in the end, it is more than likely that they all, nobles, modest artisans and marginals, served the rich merchant bourgeoisie – and *their* aims were in no way turned towards the past – as a pressure group.

We know that gradually, partly because of the skill of the regent, the future Charles V, partly because of the alliance the provost, who used every means to attain an end, made with the Jacques (a new tactical force which Marcel wished to make use of), and partly because of the unpopularity of his ally, Charles the Bad, whom public opinion reproached for his agreements with the invader (nascent national feeling worked against the provost), Marcel lost most of his allies, one after the other. Even part of the rich business bourgeoisie abandoned him and was at the root of his assassination on 31 July 1358. After some consideration, it put its loyalty to the monarchy and its hatred of the English who were pillaging the surrounding countryside above its desire to become in its turn a political elite. In future, most of the business bourgeoisie were not to take any active part in the government itself, apart from some exceptions, obviously, and excluding the money-changers who, in the following century, were to move from their banks to the finance offices of the Valois. The elite of the notables was at least as victorious as the regent, Charles.

Although a 'reformist' current was, nevertheless, to persist in France, particularly in Paris, up to the proconsulate of Bedford, and although there were riots on several occasions, as in 1380–1382 the upper merchant bourgeoisie did not play a prominent part in all this, all the more so since the provostship of the merchants had been suppressed following the troubles at the start of Charles VI's reign. But at the start of the fifteenth century another stratum wanted to accede to the rank of ruling elite. This was clearly seen when the quarrelling between the Armagnacs and Burgundians, in essence partly political, shook the capital. So the butchers took over from the drapers of the middle of the preceding century. The Saint-Yons, the Legoix, the Guérins, etc., all very rich, speculated in meat, the consumption of which was increasing in Paris as in every other city. They had many varlets, including flayers, were influential, and did not suffer (far from it!) from growing material difficulties like the mass of the poor people, the unemployed and immigrants, etc., whom they were able to rouse in order to serve their own ends. Their ambition was clear: the butchers did not command the social respect which they desired (they were not even considered a really dominant elite); they suffered because of it and, by way of compensation, wanted to take part in political decisions concerning not just the city but the entire country. In the mounting tension which seized Paris, especially after the assassination of Louis of Orleans on 23 November 1407, and with the expectation that danger would soon strike again from outside, it was easy to rouse the Parisians, just as it was to be later during the Revolution: with the least rumour, with the appearance of the most insignificant agitator, the Parisian poor and those in modest circumstances turned into rioters. From 1411, street demonstrations and hubs of insurrection multiplied. This happened all the more since the duke of Burgundy, John the Fearless, in order to obtain the lasting support (which he got) of the Parisians against the Armagnacs, made many demagogical promises under colour of reformism. As under Etienne Marcel, the Estates General, which met again in January 1413, served as a platform for calls to revolt, especially when, following tactics which had already proved their worth, they in their turn called for the dismissal of royal advisers who were considered squanderers of public money. Just as Louis XVI was to do later, the government began by giving way, but then it recalled several of these unpopular advisers, among them the provost of the provostship and viscounty, Pierre des Essarts. This was a signal to riot.

The provostship of the merchants, re-established only a short time previously, saw snatched from it, on account of a demonstration led by the butchers, the mobilization of the district militias (27 April 1413) – which inevitably make one think of the platoons of the Revolution. Although they could not take the Bastille, where Pierre des Essarts had entrenched himself, 20,000 people, according to the chroniclers, invaded the Hôtel de Guyenne in the rue Saint-Antoine, the residence of the dauphin, Louis: among the demonstrators were members of the University of Paris, including Pierre Cauchon. About fifteen people were seized and the Armagnacs were hunted throughout the night, with the benevolent neutrality of the duke of Burgundy secretly protecting the leader of the rioters, Simon Caboche – "this ignoble flayer of beasts", as the monk of Saint-Denis wrote. Until July, riots and arrests or massacres were almost daily events, especially since control of the movement seemed to have slipped from John the Fearless. But these disorders continued to serve his party which had, moreover, instigated the excellent ordinance derisively called 'Caboche's Ordinance': apart from articles destined to simplify the administration, it included a few measures in favour of the poor (against abuses of seignorial rights and of hunting, and against the illogicalities of the law, etc.).

As at the end of the Terror, the population finally tired of the constant violence, and the artisans, who had at first helped the rioters, became anxious about the serious decline in business. Powerful bourgeois, who had done scarcely anything up till now, drew nearer to the Armagnacs under the leadership of Jean Jouvenel des Ursins, one of the king's advocates. There were demonstrations against the reign of terror. On 4 August a counter-demonstration led by the butchers failed miserably, and the Armagnacs, back in Paris, organized an extremely severe repression, which goes some way towards explaining the reappearance in strength of the Burgundians some five years later. This time, in 1418, Caboche was out of it . . . he was by now one of the duke of Burgundy's officers. The riot, organized by the sinister executioner, Capeluche, served Anglo-Burgundian political interests only; it did very little for the aspirations of the butchers. These, in short, had failed in their ambitions. Although they remained potential rioters, they did not become a new ruling elite, political or otherwise. Suffice it to say that the notables remained the only French political elite. The end of the Hundred Years War was to change nothing, nor were the authoritarian monarchies of Charles VII or Louis XI.

CHAPTER 3

Rebellions linked to crisis situations

Many rebellions do not call into question the very foundations of society – unlike millenarian movements – nor do they spring from the desire of some stratum or other to improve its classification in the social hierarchy in order to accede to the rank of elite. Peasant 'terrors' and also urban movements instigated by the lower strata, thus especially by journeymen and apprentices, fall into this category. The rebellions are often seen as revolts against poverty, which is in part quite true, although not sufficient as an explanation. For the participants may take part either in their capacity as poor people, or as farmers or wage earners, or perhaps as subjects of a prince or the king, or indeed as citizens of a town.

Revolt breaks out, as we know, when what has hitherto been accepted and endured is suddenly seen as becoming unacceptable and intolerable. At such a time, social tensions, which are inherent in all societies, turn into open, brutal and violent conflicts. Does this mean that the entire social order is thus called into question? The men who went on strike at the end of the Middle Ages did not necessarily dream of bringing about a complete social upheaval, any more than do many of our contemporaries. And when they went from striking to rioting, and from there to rebellion, they became insurgents but not revolutionaries. In general, we are talking here of true revolts, thus particularly 'reactionary' revolts which turned towards the past and looked for a return to the old ways which were judged less harsh, more bearable. We are dealing with the crisis situation, whether it be economic, social or political in origin.

The fourteenth and the beginning of the fifteenth century witnessed many revolts, since a long period of economic expansion, phase A, was followed by a depression, phase B, which started in some areas with the 1315–16 wheat crisis. This reversal of the economic situation was to last, in some areas at least, for almost one and a half centuries. The consequence was a social depression, first of all in some country districts which were stricken by the continuing weakness of cereal prices and which had not gone over to some other form of cultivation that had remained profitable, then in the towns where a frequent depression in certain areas of business (for example, the textile industry in the large towns of the Low Countries) lowered the standard of living of the poorest and made them fear for their livelihood. And this social depression was made even worse by political difficulties, for instance by a reversal of the political situation, such as happened in certain regions and even entire kingdoms, particularly in France. Civil and foreign wars disrupted the circulation of men and commodities and brought destruction, famine, waves of migrant population and a feeling of insecurity. The states – cities, principalities, kingdoms – needed to obtain more money in order to wage war, but at a time when most of the population had fewer resources at its disposal. So taxation became harsher and increasingly difficult to bear, and of course increasingly unpopular. If one cannot say that there was something of a reversal in the climatic situation, one can certainly speak of a reversal in the health situation. And what a reversal! Epidemics raged, of which many, particularly the Black Death, were killers.

With some rebellions, however, it is not enough to say they are bound up with the crisis situation of the time. Although the heaviness of the taxes is bound up with the situation, the principle of taxation is closely connected to the development of the state, which is clearly a structural constant and not a contingent circumstance. Thus, any rebellion which, however vaguely, calls into question the state itself, is a 'terror' linked both to a crisis situation and to a political structure. But this is not true of the rest.

Peasant disturbances

Rural revolts do not occur in isolation. As Mousnier has written, "peasants revolt along with many others, and after many others". It is probably better to avoid calling all these revolts *Jacqueries*: the term only goes back to the fourteenth century in France and not all the peasant movements had the same causes, the same characteristics or the same development as the Ile-de-France Jacquerie of 1358. In particular, the anti-nobiliary aspect is not found everywhere.

Before 1300, we are particularly lacking in information on peasant uprisings. Engels, in his *Peasant War in Germany*, gives it to be understood that the "revolutionary opposition to feudalism was alive throughout the entire Middle Ages". But the "peasant–plebeian opposition" seemingly appeared "according to conditions of the time, either in the form of mysticism, of open heresy, or of armed insurrection". In fact, to see the mystical movements and heresies as, above all, the expression of a peasant – and urban – opposition to society as a whole, is to misunderstand the medieval mentality: this is true only in millenarian upheavals. The rural world did not exist for more than a thousand years in a state of social secession. There is little written evidence of disturbances during the first part of the Middle Ages: the peasant groups were too small and too isolated from each other for a disturbance to break out and develop geographically. We know that conditions changed considerably after 1000 with the clearing of land for cultivation, a rise in the population and economic growth, one of the major characteristics of which was an increasingly active circulation of men, materials and ideas. So that around 1300, the Western world was 'full', almost all the places inhabited at present having come into being at that time: if one were to climb the village steeple, one would see several other steeples.

How far was the improvement in the lot of the peasant and the gradual disappearance of serfdom in many regions, especially in the twelfth and thirteenth centuries, the result of planned, although not necessarily violent, movements? Historians have not yet drawn up a full list of such movements. But here is an example taken from Marc Bloch. In 1250–1, the serfs of Orly, to the south of Paris, refused to pay a tax (*taille*) which the canons of Notre-Dame had decided to levy on them: it was still the period of the 'arbitrary tax', when the total amount and the dates it was due were not fixed. People from neighbouring villages came to the aid of the recalcitrants and soon 2,000 peasants were "bonded together" against their lords. The cathedral chapter then had sixteen ringleaders imprisoned. But Blanche of Castile intervened: responding to the appeal made by the men of Orly, she offered to allow the royal tribunals to arbitrate in the dispute. After some bargaining, the canons had to give up their right to levy the arbitrary tax and, in 1263, serfdom itself was abolished at Orly. If the Middle Ages, unlike Antiquity, did not see any 'servile' wars, it was not just because the serfs were very different from the slaves of Antiquity nor because their lot was incomparably less harsh. It was also because princes and kings, far from being mere executive agents of the "ruling and exploiting class", were quite often able to act as genuine arbitrators between the social strata. Moreover, many lords realized that it was in their interests to authorize the ending of serfdom and arbitrary taxes – at least in most regions.

That there is much documentation about peasant disturbances only from the fourteenth century onwards is not just a matter of chance, but due to the fact that the depression which began at that time was one of the major causes of these 'terrors'. Their general outline, which is found again in the early modern period, is simple, displaying recurrent spatial and temporal features. The explosion is sudden, unexpected, destructive and almost always short-lived. It does, however, beg several questions. The first concerns its extent: did it have one or several epicentres? Where and how did it spread? Except, perhaps, for the English uprising in 1381, nobody has tried to compile maps tracing the progress and spread of a disturbance, as was done for the Great Fear of 1789. There is also the problem of the frequency and intensity of the disturbances in a given region. Charting frequency against intensity could on occasions lead, so Baechler believes, to the detecting of hot, luke-warm and cold phases.

We shall leave to one side the case where peasants rise against new masters. This is still fairly rare at the end of the Middle Ages, except in Scandinavia and in regions occupied by the English during the Hundred Years War. The unrest in Normandy after Agincourt, proves, moreover, that in that particular case it was not a question of a purely peasant movement: the nobles – although not the high clergy – played a large part in the affair at the head of their tenants, whether they had remained in the region or returned in secret.

The peasantry did not rise up in its entirety in any given region. At least, it would seem not. What is meant by the term *peasant* revolt is, in fact, a disturbance where the peasants constituted the major part of the insurgent manpower and where the causes of the disturbance affected mainly, in theory, the peasant world. Thus we shall not dwell on movements in which, from the start, the rustics were used by other social strata as a tactical force.

Certain difficulties peculiar to the peasantry had appeared even before 1300, thus without waiting for the end of a long period of prosperity. They were due, in particular, to the overcrowding of the countryside, which was almost general before the end of the thirteenth century. Others were peculiar to specific regions. In England, there had quite frequently been a deterioration in relations between tenants and lords, especially ecclesiastic lords, throughout the thirteenth century: contrary to what was happening at that time almost everywhere on the continent, forced labour – but only, it seems, in the great estates of the Church – had become harder and villeinage remained very widespread; the villeins were compelled to perform duties which had not been fixed by custom and they were unable to dispose either of their lands or their live-stock. Nevertheless, nothing very violent happened in the West, even in England, before the 1315–17 famine.

(A) The uprising in Maritime Flanders (1323–1328)

Pirenne has proved that the revolt which shook Bruges and Ypres for several years was led by relatively well-off peasants, not by the poor. At first, mobs had gathered in the villages, then castellans and some of the count's officers had been set upon. As these sorts of incidents were to happen more and more frequently, the movement reached the two neighbouring towns, and Bruges even took the lead in the movement. As the first of the great uprisings to erupt in a rural milieu (rare documents discovered since Pirenne's excellent study scarcely modify his analysis), it caused a considerable stir: even the great chronicler Giovanni Villani used it as a point of comparison for the Florentine disturbances.

This insurrection was undoubtedly the consequence of one of the famines which struck Europe again from 1315; the Continuator of Guillaume de Nangis points out that the two previous years had seen all sorts of climatic disasters (droughts, storms, severe cold, etc.) resulting in bad harvests and making the spring of 1324, in particular, a difficult one to tide over. Now, and this apparent coincidence was often going to be repeated up to the end of the eighteenth century, the count of Flanders, who was badly in need of money, increased taxation: this move was all the more unwise as trade was in a bad way and unemployment was severe. It was the rejection of this taxation – and also of the ecclesiastical tithe – that started the rebellion. Those peasants who were supposed to pay the taxes – that is, in the first instance, fairly well-to-do peasants – assembled to the sound of bells, soon to be followed by the fullers and weavers of Bruges and Ypres.

The terror in Maritime Flanders differs in several ways from later terrors. Firstly, because of its duration. Secondly, because it had at its head true leaders taken from among the rich landowners: there was a lord (of Sijsele), who was the military leader, and wealthy tenant-farmers such as Nicolas Zannekin and Jacques Peyte. On the other hand, recently discovered texts show that there were quite a number of day-labourers in the ranks of the insurgents, who went as far as to form a sort of administrative centre – thanks to their leaders – in the insurgent district. For blame was cast on anyone who had some position of authority, on the fiscal collectors at first, but also on other of the count's officers, echevins, clerics, even lords. Yet although Jacques Peyte loudly protested his hatred of all forms of hierarchy, the other leaders do not seem to have gone as far in this direction. As for the poorer peasants, they seem, despite the fact that their numbers were greater than Pirenne had thought, to have been scarcely more than tools manipulated by the well-to-do insurgents.

There was much verbal violence on both sides. Pillaging, burning and killing were carried out both by the insurgents – the *Karls* – and by the supporters of the threatened count and nobles, each side encouraging its followers with calls to violence. One of these calls has even come down to us: it is a song, the *Kerelslied*, in which the nobles scoff at the Karls. It needed outside intervention to bring it all to an end: avenging Courtrai and the Golden Spurs, the king of France, who had been appealed to by the count, crushed the insurgents at Cassel on 23 August 1328. Thus was ended in bloodshed "such a great and dangerous tumult – so the *Chronique de Flandre* says – as had not been seen for centuries".

(B) The Ile-de-France Jacquerie (May–June 1358)

Here, on the other hand, are some very short *terrors* – of a few weeks' duration only – whose characteristics are quite different from the above. They were, however, just as serious.

It would be as absurd to paint an idyllic picture of relations between the lord and his tenants around the year 1300, as to describe them as being at each other's throats, even in the manors of certain English lords who have been called 'warring lords'. The bond between the master and his peasants was not just a means whereby the powerful could exploit the weak. More often than not, in fact, the powerful considered themselves responsible for the lot of their peasants: despite the growth of the royal or princely power, they remained the peasants' natural protectors, and they quite often acted as such, particularly in face of the fiscal demands of the state. And the peasants were fully aware that it was in their interests to have the most powerful lord they could, so as to protect them from excessively heavy taxation and over-zealous tax-collectors: and again, in Colbert's time, it was to be said that the peasants least burdened by taxation were those attached to the most powerful lords.

But in the fourteenth century, the age of unrest, which had seemed over for generations, was reborn. Public authority and order took a beating and there was an increase in brigand lords in France, Germany and Italy. And the prestige of the nobleman declined: in England at first, then in France, the army lost some of its 'feudal' aspect and the 'soldiers' became rivals of the knights. The lord often lost his officering role over his own men, indeed his very power to command them. Now, in France, this decline in the prestige of the noble was more accentuated than elsewhere because the knights were beaten, several times, by archers or mere foot-soldiers. The defeat of the knights at Courtrai prefigured Crécy and Poitiers. After this last defeat in 1356 particularly, the chivalry, in the eyes of public opinion, seemed to have lost its *raison d'être*, which was to defend the kingdom and all its inhabitants, especially, of course, the king.

This happened at a time when circumstances caused a reduction in the revenue of the nobles, who were very short of money. In addition, people had to contribute to their lord's ransom if he had been taken prisoner at Poitiers, not to mention the ransom for the king himself. All these factors would indicate that the tax-farmers or collectors of seignorial taxes were becoming more insistent and more rigorous in claiming their dues. It will be remembered, too, that the chosen terrain of the Jacquerie was that part of the Ile-de-France which was bare of vines, that is, where there was little to alleviate the effects of the prolonged slump in cereal prices. And the collective nervousness, a result of the Black Death about ten years previously, had certainly not abated. In any case, it was the most populated areas, those where the soil was best (despite the fact there were no vines), which were to rise up, not the poor districts: the Jacquerie just cannot be explained as a "terrible awakening from poverty".

The term *Jacquerie* enjoyed great popularity for a long time. The chronicler, Jean le Bel, had mistakenly said that Jacques Bonhomme (it was, in fact, Guillaume Cale) was the leader of the insurgents. In future the French were to think of the insurgent peasants as *Jacques* . . . until the far-off day, that is, when the term *Croquants* was to take over . . .. The lasting success of the name is a fair indication of the great impression the 1358 revolt made on the collective mentality.

Although – and this was rare – knowledge of these 'terrors' was not restricted to those involved (the mendicant monk, Jean de Venette, understood the peasants' grievances, as did the Norman, the author of the *Chronique des quatre premiers Valois*), exactly what it was that seemed to become totally unbearable for the villagers remains a matter of conjecture. One could probably put forward at least two more or less immediate causes. One of them was the pillaging by the men-at-arms (both regulars and irregulars) after the entry into the Ile-de-France, around November–December 1357, of gangs of Anglo-Navarrese who, according to Froissart, "were day by day conquering and laying waste the entire region between the Loire and the Seine". The other cause lay both in the fiscal demands of the monarchy, in desperate straits since the defeat at Poitiers, and the recriminations of the Estates General which, between 1355 and 1357, found a more sympathetic welcome in the countryside near the capital than elsewhere. Seeing their resources dwindle more and more, and feeling threatened by the Companies, the peasants thus rose both against lords and the fisc, which seemed unjustly rigorous at a time when the orators of the Estates were making much of all the governmental squandering.

The main seat of insurrection, probably the first but not the only one, was at Saint-Leu-d'Esserent, near Creil, on the border of the Parisian region, although at the same time quite clearly inside it. People were wrong to think, as they did for such a long time, that the peasants in districts closer to Paris rebelled only later, at the instigation of Etienne Marcel. The area covered by the uprising was both more extensive and came closer to the capital. And it had several starting-points. Unless we are mistaken, we are the first to have compared this Jacquerie to the Great Fear of 1789: although it would be foolish to push the comparison too far, the fact remains that both had several points of origin and several relay-points, although one cannot say whether this is explained by the underground activity of agitators or by the almost simultaneous occurrence of 'nervous' outbursts, such as those studied by sociologists concerned with the pathology of the crowd. As far as the Jacquerie is concerned, it is quite probable that, although spontaneous at first, the *terrors* were then very soon aggravated, extended and exploited by the rich merchant bourgeoisie in Paris and by a small group of ambitious royal officers who wanted to "fish in troubled waters". Amongst the starting-points one may count Saint-Leu (for certain), but also Montmorency and Vémars out in the Plaine de France, the area around Pontoise – which would have served as an intermediate point between the south-east of the Beauvaisis and the north of Paris – and Longjumeau to the south of Paris. Even if there was spontaneity in the beginning, the activity of Cale, "captain of the Beauvaisis" (not a very accurate term), was soon conspicuous in co-ordinating the bands of Jacques. He became a sort of symbol of revolt and its organizer, sending emissaries out into the villages which had remained apart from the unrest: the spreading of the disturbance owed much to him. On their own account or at Cale's request, the villagers of each parish chose a 'captain', such as Jacquin de Chennevières, who was the choice at Taverny near Montmorency: as elsewhere, the inhabitants had first asked the royal provost for instructions, and he (not the only officer to act in such a way) let the Jacques do as they pleased, possibly with his tacit approval.

The violence of the revolt was both severe and short-lived. It had begun about 28 May and was put down in bloodshed at Mello on 9 June, at the very time when other peasants, who had joined together with Parisians, were being defeated at Meaux, the refuge of the close associates of the duke of Normandy. For the nobles, who were the prime targets of the insurgents (who did not attack the clergy), had very quickly pulled themselves together. And the more or less forced alliance between the Jacques and the followers of Etienne Marcel had not sorted out the affairs of the peasants, whom the provost of the merchants had encouraged to help the insurgent burghers against the royal officers who had remained loyal to the regent.

Jean le Bel and Froissart, amongst others, have recorded aspects of this violent insurrection of villagers who assembled to the call of bells, roused possibly by popular orators who travelled the countryside; they were "without armour other than iron sticks and knives". The letters of remission granted shortly afterwards to the main culprits corroborate the most adverse of contemporary statements. There were horrific scenes; but, of course, it was pillaging, especially the destruction of fortified houses, which was the most frequent occurrence. And all this happened in some two weeks . . .. If the number of insurgents did not run into tens of thousands, it at least ran into thousands. But since the Ile-de-France had an exceptionally dense population, it comes down to saying that the majority of the peasants (which – the poorest or the rest?) seemingly took no part in the 'terrors'.

After the Jacquerie came the Counter-Jacquerie, in other words the repression led by the nobles, and not by the state, which in any case had very little power. The nobles began a campaign of brutal, bloody reprisals. On the eve of the battle of Mello, Cale, we know, was trapped by Charles the Bad in an ambush. After the defeat of his troops, he was beheaded, whilst those of his men who had escaped from Mello were caught and massacred. As for the citizens of Meaux, allies of the Jacques, they paid dearly for their rebellion: the mayor was put to death, the inhabitants killed or held to ransom, and the town (apart from the cathedral) was burned to the ground. The nobles roamed the countryside: Jean de Venette tells of the severity of their action, especially when

Charles the Bad was no longer with them to act as a moderating influence. But Etienne Marcel exaggerates a good deal when he describes the Counter-Jacquerie as a "war of extermination" and compares the nobles to the Vandals or the Saracens. Verbal threats, acts of cruelty and pillaging were far more common than murder.

The monarchy was skilful. From 10 August, the future Charles V had a letter of remission read everywhere, which applied to all the insurgents – Jacques and Parisians – and to all the nobles. The regent stated in it, moreover, that some gentlemen had indeed burnt a number of peasant houses and that some of them had even gone as far as committing criminal acts. But it is not easy to know when calm was actually restored in people's minds. What is certain, however, is that for some years nobles took judicial action against peasants in order to obtain heavy indemnities. But fortunately, public opinion, which was made up of groups formerly opposed to each other, soon suffered a distraction: danger from the shady intrigues of the king of Navarre and, even more, from fresh English incursions, with Edward III's men-at-arms appearing in the province once again from 1360. One would like to know the effects of this sudden outburst of violence on the relations between those lords and peasants who had confronted one another. What was daily life like, and what happened when the taxes were being collected? Order was certainly re-established, but when, how and to what extent?

There was no flagrant animosity against the nobles in general during subsequent movements which were, it seems, supported by fewer peasants. The nobles, now more experienced and less maladroit after the 1358 'terrors', the memory of which stayed with them for a long time, were generally able to resume their ancestral role by defending, as far as was possible, their men against mercenary bands and sometimes even against merchants. Moreover, the subsequent disturbances had a different aspect and developed differently. In the early days, whenever they were dissatisfied with a lord who, because of a general lack of means, did not seem very capable of protecting them against the havoc wrought by troops (regular or otherwise), the Ile-de-France rustics would ask the royal provost for the authority to form self-defence groups. Armed with old swords, wooden bows and, of course, spiked clubs, the *piquiers* hid in the woods in order to surprise their enemies while they pillaged on horseback. But later, these armed peasants did not distinguish between friendly and hostile troops. Then they set ambushes on the roads and the number of pillagers swelled. They were called *Brigands* around 1417, that is, at the time when the war with the English, coming on top of the civil struggles between the Armagnacs and the Burgundians, began to rage once again. After Charles VII's victory in Paris in 1436, and because the royal troops, who were badly paid and too few in number, were unable to sweep the Parisian region clean, a similar phenomenon occurred. According to Thomas Basin, peasants and other irregulars "were flaying everything", hence the nickname *Ecorcheurs* which contemporaries gave them. Only the complete liberation of the Ile-de-France in 1441 was to put an end to the violence which, moreover, had not really been of the 'protest' kind on a social or economic level – a point supported by the fact that many nobles had joined these bands and some of them often acted as their leaders.

The movements experienced by other regions of France should be distinguished from the 1358 Jacquerie, for they had more in common with the true brigandism of marginals to whom they were closer even than the bands of Ile-de-France *Brigands*. The two best known movements at the end of the fourteenth century are the Tuchins, who long terrorized the southern regions of France, and the *Chaperons blancs* of Normandy. In the fifteenth century, the Burgundian *Coquillards* rivalled the *Ecorcheurs*. And so on. One cannot say that these marginals were just following the example of the pillaging men-at-arms, since tax evasion played an important part. But, as hatred of society as a whole, not only of the lords, also played its part in the outburst, extent and duration of these disturbances, the problem could be a question of anti-societies which, exceptionally, were not messianic. In any case, some nobles did not hesitate to join in with, or even sometimes to be the instigators of, these 'terrors', which were profitable because of increased pillaging and ransom demands. Once again, we maintain that vertical solidarity was stronger than horizontal solidarity.

(C) The English Peasants' Revolt of 1381

The English Peasants' Revolt of 1381 is as famous as the 1358 Jacquerie. It occurred, moreover, during a period of keen unrest almost everywhere in the West, in both country and town. At the time, the Tuchins movement doubled in strength and some cities, such as Rouen and Paris, saw much bloodshed. French historians are wrong when they speak of a 'workers' revolt', as if artisans and peasants had all risen up at the same time and without the help of other social categories. R. B. Dobson has recently brought this home to us most forcefully.

Peasants rarely rose up on their own. For the bonds between the towns, especially the small ones, and the country districts were too close for the inhabitants of the minor towns not to have acted immediately like the country dwellers. Meaux, Corbeil and Melun, for example, had taken part in the 1358 'terrors'. Similarly, the 1381 rising involved the inhabitants of Canterbury, Norwich, Yarmouth, Bury St Edmunds, Ipswich, St Albans, Winchester and Bridgwater. But there seems to have been one distinct difference between the 1358 'terrors' and those of 1381: the role of the lower clergy was minimal in the Ile-de-France of 1358; in England it was of prime importance, as was shown by the actions of a John Ball or a John Wrawe, who moved the crowds to mass hysteria. There was another difference: it would be wrong to see an anti-nobiliary movement in the 1381 rebellion, despite Ball's famous text against the 'gentleman' and the fact that some lords did suffer in the revolt. At the time, the smallest landlords were victims of the economic depression and the labour shortage arising from depopulation: temporarily, in some areas of eastern England (as a little later in the Hussite movement), an alliance was formed between the richer peasantry and the lesser squirarchy. But there were other factors which demonstrate once again the strength of vertical solidarity: the great majority of the gentlemen who took part in the uprising were encouraged to do so by the collapse of the state and of order during the summer of 1381. Real 'gentry gangs', so Dobson writes, took advantage of the collapse to extend the range of certain of their somewhat shady, indeed 'protection racket', activities. Other knights or squires were unable to resist pressure from their neighbours or kinsfolk: Sir William Coggan felt obliged, on pain of losing his position as a 'good lord', to join the "conspiracy" hatched by the vicar and other rebels in Bridgwater. Finally (and it is not the only rebellion to evoke the war in the Vendée during the Revolution), it is certain that many peasants felt the need to be commanded by members of the gentry who were experienced in warfare. This is why the insurgents so rarely attacked secular lords. Indeed, the death of one of them, Robert Salle, who was killed by the Norfolk rebels, is attributable to the fact that he had refused to join in with them.

It is impossible to see anything in this rebellion which can be interpreted as a class struggle. We know that the English peasantry was a particularly variegated body. One should not think that the depression and depopulation had had the effect of reducing the number of peasant strata to two, that of the 'kulaks' and that of the 'proletarians'. Amongst the insurgents there were both very wealthy peasants and others who suffered badly from the depression. Moreover, despite the exceptional wealth of source material relative to these 'terrors', one cannot be sure whether whole village communities rebelled or not.

Since rich or fairly well-off people rebelled, one cannot advance as the sole cause of the rebellion the seignorial reaction which had raged in the great estates since the thirteenth century. The fiscal causes are more important because they are more general: they affected the poor as well as the well-off. One can also say that the uprising was a backlash against the defeats in France suffered by the aged Edward III and then the young King Richard: the French had by now retaken almost all the land lost in 1360 and, although they were now losing some impetus, they still had to be contained; thus English and Gascon troops had to be raised and equipped, and thus taxes had to be levied, which were all the heavier since the war on the continent no longer brought in profitable spoils as it had done previously.

The 1377 parliament had chosen to levy a capitation, the poll-tax, of four pence from every person, both male and female, over the age of fourteen. It was rather unfair, even though beggars were exempt; but at least the rate was low. Two years later, it tried to impose another tax, where the rate, this time, was proportional to one's wealth. But this was a failure. So in 1380 the uniform rate was reverted to, but treble that of 1377 (one shilling per head), payable by each person over the age of fifteen, beggars excepted. Depending on the number of its inhabitants, each community was taxed a global sum; it could then divide the total amount between its members, but proportionately, in accordance with the means of each person. Many villeins still paid one shilling each, a sum equivalent to three days' wages for a labourer, and which was higher than all previous taxes. Besides, according to the best source the *Anonimalle chronicle*, the men who had ordered the imposition of this tax were already unpopular in the country, among them the young king's uncle, John of Gaunt, duke of Lancaster: as far as public opinion was concerned, the king's advisers were traitors, and the best proof of this was that the French were now victorious.

At the beginning of 1381, as the collecting of the new tax went on, so the discontent increased. The constables in the communities had to close their eyes to innumerable frauds, and the taxable population fell to two-thirds that of 1377. But the royal council reacted by ordering an inquiry which was to begin on 16 March and take in fifteen counties. The commissioners entrusted with the inquiry uncovered considerable evasion which involved thousands of tax-payers in quite small towns . . ..

With the announcement of these inspections, and at the appearance of the investigators, the discontent doubled. On 30 May in Essex, a commissioner who was not protected by men-at-arms had to flee in the face of the rustics' resistance. Within a few days, the whole of Essex and Kent were involved in the revolt, manors were stormed, and 7 June saw Wat Tyler at the head of a large host. Then more manors were taken and their archives destroyed. On 10 June Canterbury was invaded, the archbishop's palace was pillaged, the county archives were burnt, and Wat Tyler, who had just been taken prisoner, was freed.

If, during the first phase, the rebels rose only against the fiscal agents, it is clear that later they attacked wealthy lords, and especially ecclesiastics. Probably under the influence of popular preachers, of whom the most famous is John Ball, and of Wat Tyler, whose aims were perhaps already revolutionary, certain powerful men came under attack, as did monks belonging to rich abbeys, rich merchants and foreigners. The insurgents were not satisfied with burning manorial archives (as they were in France in 1789), but they demanded from the lords, especially from the clerics, charters of collective or individual 'manumissions', fairly similar to those which many French peasants had obtained, but generally without violence, in the previous century.

On 11 and 12 June the ever-increasing number of insurgents (although probably not as many as the 50,000 claimed by the *Anonimalle chronicle*) marched on London. Within the city, where the mayor, Walworth, was determined to resist, many inhabitants, and not only guildsmen, were in sympathy with the insurgents. On the evening of 12 June the bands met up, reached the suburbs, and pillaged the bishop's palace. Confusion was now at its height in the entourage of the king, only fourteen years old. As the peasants had no food, they had to enter the city: on 13 June an alderman was instrumental in having the bridge lowered. On that day, rich Londoners had their houses ravaged, the palace of the unpopular John of Gaunt was set on fire, and the Temple of the Knights of St John of Jerusalem was ransacked. The leaders, one of whom was Wat Tyler, gathered at the home of a rich city-dweller who was sympathetic to the revolt (there were many such) and drew up a list of proscripts. From the Tower of London, Richard could see the fires close by which had been lit by the peasants, a sight of "great horror" (*grande hideur*) for him according to Froissart. After much hesitant deliberation in the council, the king decided to speak with the crowd on 14 June. In fact, he had to accept the demands formulated by Wat Tyler: the abolition of serfdom, a general amnesty, perhaps also the repeal of the unpopular Statute of

Labourers imposed after the Black Death, and the punishing of the 'traitors', etc. In order better to appease the insurgents, the king had chapters of freedom and amnesty drawn up.

Thus encouraged by these early successes, the insurgents attacked the Tower and killed several of their enemies. On 15 June Tyler's followers, weakened by the departure of many peasants whom the royal concessions had satisfied, confronted the king and his retinue outside the walls, at Smithfield: fresh demands were made, including one for the suppression of the Church's goods. Following a keen altercation, the mayor had Tyler struck down under the eyes of his followers. Then came the repression, led by Robert Knowles, whom the French knew to their cost as a man of war: he wanted to kill all the rebels, but Richard, who was more subtle, showed himself to be relatively moderate. But then the uprising spread: the whole of the south-east, East Anglia and other counties (Lincolnshire, Leicestershire, etc.) were affected. Troops had to be sent here, there and everywhere. It was not just the government which reacted; the bishop of Norwich, for example, raised an army of volunteer nobles who meted out severe punishment to the insurgent villages. The repression and retribution were to last into September–October (Ball had been executed at St Albans on 15 July). It goes without saying that the concessions which had been wrought from the king were revoked. But, as happened after the 1358 Jacquerie, which had not extended over such a wide area, there was soon an amnesty (on 14 November 1381), although 247 fugitives were excluded from it.

There are some points of resemblance between the 1381 and 1358 uprisings. There was the same bitterness against the royal advisers, although the king himself did not come under attack, the same hostility against the fisc, and the same understanding – limited or otherwise – between the rustics and the inhabitants of the capital. Although the Londoners' demands were of a more political nature, similar to those of the Parisians in 1358, the rebel peasants were welcome at first in both cases, especially as they represented a very useful pressure group to the city-dwellers. But some members of the London merchant bourgeoisie were victims of the events in 1381, unlike their Parisian counterparts some twenty years earlier. In both cases, on the other hand, the artisan world – journeymen and masters alike – was sympathetic to the insurgents. Neither for England nor France is there proof of any clear-cut opposition between town and countryside: even if interests diverged, this did not lead to a struggle between city-dwellers and peasants (as was fairly often the case in Flanders), even though Marx saw this as a general truth for the end of the Middle Ages.

(D) The peasant disturbances in Aragon (fifteenth century)

The most important rebellions in the fifteenth century were probably
those which occurred in Aragon. They were similar in several respects to
the English and French *terrors* outlined above, but in particular on
account of a growing hostility towards royal fiscality. In other respects
they were different: several were characterized by a hatred against the
towns on the part of the rustics, as happened in Italy: Catalan legislation
prohibited villagers from going to settle in the towns, which were
developing rapidly at the time. This was the prime cause of the first
movements, those which occurred in 1409 and the following years. On the
other hand, the next round of commotions seem to owe their explanation
rather to a strong feeling of bitterness against the nobles. We know that in
the southern countries, far from experiencing the temporary 'weakening'
which took place elsewhere, lordship became stronger and firmer. The
Peninsular lords extended the common of pasture for their huge flocks at
the expense of the rustics' flocks, and they also went as far as levying
certain dues. In Catalonia, a restlessness which had started in 1462 was to
last for a quarter of a century and then end only after royal intervention.
Indeed, the kings had set their troops against the rebels on several
occasions, for example in Majorca. One will note that, as had happened a
short time previously in England, the rebels sometimes rose against
foreigners, in this case against the settlers who had come from France.
It is possible, too, that these movements were tinged with messianism
or, at least, a certain mysticism, as was the case in England
in 1381 where Wyclif's influence, despite his efforts in the opposite
direction, was in no way negligible. In the Peninsula, this mysticism
would be connected with the preaching of St Vincent Ferrier: the
natural order had been seriously disturbed, and the balance which had
existed between rich and poor had to be restored. In other words,
here we find once again 'reactionary' revolts which looked towards
the past.

In northern Europe, rural lordship overcame its 'weakness' in the
course of the fifteenth century. It continued to exist, and often to prosper,
down to the early modern period: in France, for example, it did not die a
natural death but was put down by the 1789–1792 Revolution. Before the
appearance of the Physiocrats, at least, the country regions had
undergone scarcely any major transformations since the end of the

Middle Ages, and the peasantry itself evolved only very slowly. This is another reason for not hesitating to compare the peasant disturbances at the end of the Middle Ages with those which shook France, for example, in the seventeenth century. It should be acknowledged once again that the analyses put forward by modernists are very useful to medievalists. However, these analyses do sometimes differ. In 1948, B. F. Porchnev proposed a Marxist explanation for the popular rebellions which took place before the Fronde (1623–1648). All these movements, both rural and urban ones, occurred when new taxes were introduced or new laws created which made existing taxation heavier. Spontaneous at first, they were subsequently used, according to Porchnev, by the bourgeois and nobles. Thus, it was the 'populace', the most underprivileged sector, which first went into action. These rebellions were not anti-monarchical but were directed against the rich, the beneficiaries of 'feudal' revenue, whether the said beneficiaries profited directly as lords, indirectly on drawing their wages from the state or made handsome profits during the levying of taxes. And the peasant disturbances were bound to fail, both because they were running up against a 'class front' and because the workers were too few in number and too bereft of political ideas to manage urban and rural revolts.

Mousnier has brought out clearly the good points of Porchnev's theses, but he has also shown up the less good points. Richelieu and Mazarin (like some French or English king at the end of the Middle Ages) suspected that nobles and burghers had played a part in the instigating of rebellions – a truth which, as we have seen, holds good for the rebellions of the fourteenth and fifteenth centuries and a truth which one is liable to overlook if one insists on painting an unduly black picture of relationships between lords and tenants.

One does not find in the seventeenth century, any more than previously, *all* the rustics forming a united front against the lords, any more than one finds an alliance of *all* the owning and ruling strata, in short the elites, against the rustics. The following quotation from Mousnier fits the end of the Middle Ages as well as it does the seventeenth century: "Most of the lords thus protected their men against the fisc or against passing troops or those billeted nearby. They intervened in matters involving royal officers, brought about reductions in the tallage paid by their peasants and won them exemptions from tolls and forced labour. In times of trouble they armed their tenants and farmers, formed leagues of mutual assistance and made sure the livestock and crops of their men were respected. They organized tax resistance and stirred up the feeling of the peasants against the fisc. And they incited revolts." It is precisely when they did not behave like this that anti-nobiliary 'terrors' broke out, in the fourteenth and fifteenth centuries just as in the seventeenth century.

In France, at least, lords and tenants had other interests in common at the end of the Middle Ages. Loyalty to the monarchy and hatred of the English brought nobles and rustics closer together – or sometimes even reconciled them completely. Thus, in 1410, all the "male subjects and inhabitants" of the barony of Le Neubourg in Normandy took part in the restoration and equipping of the château, "as much with their bodies as with their horses and other beasts drawing plough or cart". John III of Le Neubourg acknowledged in writing that they had done this "of their own free will, without any coercion", "for the good and safety of their persons, possessions, wives and children, *and for the public good of the whole country*". One would be very wrong to consider the château as the hereditary enemy of the peasant cottages: for everyone it was a place of defence and refuge and, even in quiet times, an indispensable meeting-place for the villagers, as has just been demonstrated once again for the county of Tonnerre. Let the danger resurface – wrote A. Plaisse in relation to Le Neubourg – and the bond uniting one man with the next will rediscover all its old meaning: "The peasant helps the lord whose *man* he is because he expects protection from him and also . . . because he holds him in a certain amount of esteem." This explains why, when people rose against a lord who did not fulfil his obligations, they did not demand the suppression of the seignorial institution, but another, more capable, lord. This fact has just been demonstrated by H. Platelle with regard to Saint-Amand in Pévèle. There was keen discontent in this border area, which was under the control of the bailiff of Vermandois, following fiscal rulings by the 1355 Estates General (a tax of eight pence per pound on all sales and a salt tax). The people wanted the abbot of Saint-Amand to call together the community of the town and surrounding area so that in his capacity as lord he could protect them against the collecting of the salt tax (February 1356). He refused, telling the agitated population that they should pay "without trouble". The inhabitants revolted and tried to prevent the eventual entry of the king's agents. At the instigation of one of the inhabitants, who seems to have been the leader in the whole affair, the people, in a state of turmoil, gathered together in a church in July 1356. *Habemus dominum* [the abbot] *qui non custodit nec deffendit nos*, they declared: they were strongly critical of the prelate for not protecting his men against the fisc and the royal law. At the instigation of their leader, the inhabitants decided to see a Tournai advocate; they wanted him to draw up in their name a list of demands to present to the abbot and have him advised that in the event of his refusing them they would seek another lord (*nisi omnia ad debitum finem perducaret juxta eorum dicta, alium dominum requirerent*). Everything quietened down it seems – but we do not know the final act of this rebellion which one supposes came to an abrupt end; the fact remains that the inhabitants had clearly thought of choosing another lord, the nearby count of Hainaut who, indeed, would have carried more weight in face of the fiscal demands of the Valois.

To return to the example of Normandy, one will recall, too, the attitude of the peasantry towards the 'intruders', lords whom the occupiers had installed in the place of the lawful lords who were faithful to Charles VII and had been dispossessed of their lands. If the rustics tried their hardest not to pay dues to the new masters, it was not just because of national feeling, but also because they did everything possible to try and get these dues to their lawful masters who were not very far away, since the 'Armagnac' zone bordered on southern Normandy: the English occupation had not broken the feudal bond and, at the risk of their lives, the rustics managed to keep in touch with their former lords. When these lords returned after the English had left, it is clear that this bond, which had just come so well through a difficult test, was to continue to be. This is why the 'peasant' revolts were always limited in their strength and, almost always, in their scope: the bond did not break everywhere, or when it did, it was not broken for long.

Urban disturbances

According to the Marxists, the "general crisis in feudalism" in the fourteenth and fifteenth centuries was accompanied by an increase in class conflict in the towns. It is true that social tensions were more pronounced at that time than previously. But was this linked to the structures of society? It was far more probably linked to the crisis situation of the moment, which made old problems worse and caused an upsurge of new ones. And social promotion at the time often seemed blocked to the lower strata of the urban population.

In his *Peasant War in Germany*, Engels very rightly insisted on the increase in the number of marginals, whom he calls the *Lumpenproletariat*. What Engels saw as the plebeian opposition in the towns consisted of "budding proletarian elements" in addition to these marginals. "On the one hand," – he continues – "impoverished artisans who, because of their privileges, still clung to the existing middle-class order; on the other hand, ejected peasants and ex-officials who were yet unable to become proletarians. Between these two groups were the journeymen, for the time being outside official society (?) and as close to the standard of living of the proletariat as the industry of the times and the guild privileges would permit, but, due to the same privileges, almost all prospective middle-class master artisans" (not often true any more, we know, at the end of the Middle Ages). Basically – and by saying so Engels shows himself to be more subtle than many of his followers – there was not a single 'proletarian' uprising, not even in an embryonic form, before the Peasant's War in Luther's time. Engels even pointed out quite clearly the often 'reactionary' elements which, even at the end of the Middle Ages, were present in the urban disturbances where the plebeian opposition played the primary role: "a shouting, rapacious tail-end to the middle-class opposition, a mob that could be bought and sold for a few barrels of wine" – he adds scornfully – . . . "it demanded extension of city trade privileges over the rural districts, and it did not like to see the city revenues curtailed by abolition of feudal burdens in the rural area belonging to the city." On these points there was complete agreement between the poor and the rich burghers.

Engels nevertheless omitted two facts. The first concerns the more or less complete 'closing' of many guilds: since access to the mastership was, in theory, reserved for the sons of masters, the journeymen often lost all hope of rising in the social hierarchy. The second, which is linked to the first, concerns the frequent stagnation in artisan activity as a result of the depression, political difficulties and wars. The common good was forgotten and each guild, each town, wanted to prevent competition by establishing a 'protectionism'; this was bound to lead to further economic difficulties as well as to increasing bitterness in social relations.

M. Mollat and Ph. Wolff have rightly noted that the first 'cracks' appeared, in any case, before the passing from a long phase A to a phase B: they would thus be the price paid for the expansion which was not yet complete in the second half of the thirteenth century. "In northern France and the former Low Countries" – they write – "industrial and commercial expansion was still continuing when resentment against the rich manifested itself, sometimes with the help of deserters from the ruling milieu – jealous, ambitious or idealistic men – sometimes, too, within the framework, which was still embryonic, of professional or confraternal artisan associations. Among the most underprivileged the illusion prevailed that once the patriciate was brought down, roles would be reversed." The unrest, which was sporadic at first, "degenerated into simultaneous, and sometimes pre-planned, outbreaks of violence" from 1275 onwards. Sometimes the rule of the 'patricians' was attacked, together with weight of taxation which was intolerable for the poor, and sometimes the high cost of food – especially in Italy – provoked the disturbance.

A new factor, and one which Beaumanoir testifies as not being the perquisite of the Low Countries, was the strike (the French word *grève* is Parisian in origin . . .) and the co-operation between wage-earners wanting to obtain wage increases. The great jurist saw all this as "an alliance against the common profit", thus liable to fines and long terms of imprisonment. Trouble broke out in 1280 in the large cloth-manufacturing towns: at Douai the strike turned into a riot which was brutally put down, with even the death penalty being used. But striking, an innovation of the end of the thirteenth century, did not always – indeed, far from it – lead to rebellion.

(A) Early disturbances linked to dramatic changes in circumstances

Monetary changes, increasing fiscality, famines, epidemics and wars go a long way towards explaining the revolts which broke out in the greater part of the fourteenth century, especially after the start of the depression, phase B.

The monetary changes, which began around 1300 in France, were not merely unpopular. They provoked bitter discontent, with people soon realizing their effects on price/wage relations and on sums owed by debtors. Such was the case in 1306 when Philip the Fair devalued by more than a third: prices rose and creditors demanded what was owed them in hard currency, which was possible because of the simultaneous existence of money of account and real money. In Paris, the tenants who had rented their lodgings refused to do this, and they set upon the king's men who had come to support the lessors. This was something which was to happen on several occasions in the capital right up to the end of the Hundred Years War – a breeding ground for monetary manipulations. In addition, rumblings of rebellion were heard in January 1307, when blame was cast on a former provost of the merchants, Etienne Barbette, because he was master of the mint. Even the king, who had taken refuge in the Temple, was besieged by the mob, which was made up mainly of artisans. Some years later, during the Flemish troubles, the Parisian population once again reacted violently and went on a tax strike. Basically, this particular form of strike was for a long time more frequent than a work strike:

sometimes it was the royal taxes and sometimes the urban ones which were the cause of the discontent and unrest.

Famine, too, could lead to rebellion, as in Barcelona at the beginning of 1334. And if it came at the same time as an epidemic and a war, things were naturally much more serious. This happened in a number of Italian cities, such as Venice, Bologna, Florence and Siena, during the years preceding the Black Death of 1348. Fiscality seemed even more difficult to bear at such a time, and the cry of the people, as in Florence in 1343, was: "Down with taxes".

Then the 1348 epidemic struck. The survivors ran into new difficulties, which were quite incomprehensible to them. For the first time for centuries there was a labour shortage and wages rose considerably. People turned to the state – it was the first time they had done so in this connection – and kings and princes tried to find a remedy for the shortage of manpower and the inflation in wages. No solution was found in France, where at least the sovereign did not persevere. But in England, draconian measures were decreed (compulsory work, expelling of beggars, a wage freeze). The Statute of Labourers of 1351 was even harsher, since it made the sanctions previously envisaged for offenders even more severe. All this provoked great discontent, which was all the more justified since the authorities were having even less success in curbing price inflation than wage inflation .... If, for the time being, there was no revolt, relations between wage-earners and employers were none the less much embittered.

(B) The years 1378 to 1383

Historians, like contemporaries, have been struck by the large number of disturbances and rebellions in the West from the spring of 1378 to the start of 1383. But are we dealing with a movement which was both unique and general, or with the juxtaposition of several disturbances? We should not forget that alongside urban disturbances at that time, there existed rural 'terrors' (for example in England, p. 139).

In Florence, the city of the red lily, there had not been a sustained period of calm for decades. From 1340, discontent with the *popolo grasso*, high taxation, difficulties in obtaining food and the problem of wages joined with the still unsuccessful demands of the second-ranking guilds, master artisans and labourers, in the fostering of a latent uneasiness. Was the 1378 revolt just the result of this uneasiness?

The French term *'tumulte'* (the Revolt of the Ciompi = *Le tumulte des Ciompi* in French) clearly expresses the great agitation and disorder of the disturbance. Yet, if one looks only to the principal actors in the Florentine violence of the summer of 1378, the *ciompi* – that is to say the workers or *sottoposti,* some of whom were the worst paid in the textile *artisanat* – one can see the affair as being due to extreme poverty. But it did not become a revolution: the despair of the lowest strata is clearly visible, but so is the conservative nature of their demands. Economic factors, particularly the indisputable exploitation of the *sottoposti* by Florentine businessmen, cannot account fully for the disturbance. One should not exaggerate the messianic influences on the revolt either: in Florence, the Brethren of the Free Spirit as well as the Spirituals won sympathizers, but their mythic ideals found little place in the demands of the *ciompi.* On the other hand, the strength of personal bonds, formed between members of the same faction or the same clientele, is indisputable. This is not immediately evident on reading contemporary chronicles, and the role of these bonds has long been minimized in the same way that little account has been taken of the strength of the vertical solidarity existing between master artisans, journeymen and apprentices. But, basing his argument on an analysis of notarial minutes, G. A. Brucker has recently made a reassessment of the great revolt of 21 July to 31 August 1378, which accorded the lowest strata of the textile world temporary participation in the city government. Thus, the original characteristics of the revolt are being re-established through the reconstitution of the leaders' biographies, and the attitudes and actions of the *Balia,* the 'insurrectional' commission. The movement then seems typically Florentine, with personal and neighbourship bonds and membership of a faction carrying greater weight than economic motivation.

Why was it that the movement erupted in 1378? Many *sottoposti* had long lived a precarious existence; they were badly paid, and in an unreliable currency, restricted in what they could earn (maximum wage), they worked only one day in two because of the large number of feast days, were in debt and consequently a prey to the threats of the law because of their insolvency. As many of them in the textile industry did not belong to a guild, and since the right of association was denied them, they were without protection. The date of 1378 is explained by the current crisis situation: the war against the Holy See, the so-called War of the 'Eight Saints', had just shaken the city deeply. It is true that Brucker has shown that it did not bring about a serious economic depression, since merchants supplied wool and bought cloth despite the interdict placed on the town, and thus prevented a rise in unemployment and prices. But the war provoked a *political* crisis, which was the more or less immediate cause of the revolt. In addition, in the spring of 1378, the consuls of the woollen 'art' had just made social promotion more difficult by quadrupling the matriculation tax and thus denying journeymen at the top of the *sottoposti* category almost all hope of acceding to the status of *lanaioli*. We know that such stratagems were common at the time in the West. The resulting tension was made even worse by a host of political proscriptions.

Now, on 1 May 1378, Salvestro de' Medici entered the signoria as gonfalonier of justice. Benefiting from the intolerance of the Guelph party's captains who accused two artisans of Ghibellinism, he created for himself a clientele made up of the poor and weak, of artisans too, and even of merchants. The explosion came on 18 June, after a theatrical outburst during which Salvestro attacked the tyranny of the rich and of the signoria. Four days later the rioters set fire to palaces, then attacked convents. Out of xenophobia and a dread of unemployment, foreigners were hanged (possibly Flemish workers in the textile industry).

The signoria had to make concessions, promise a purge and sanctions against powerful persons, and undertake to re-examine the position of outlaws. But concessions very rarely put an end to a revolt. And this revolt re-erupted with increased strength and fury on 8 July, following a petition in which the minor 'arts' demanded that there should be civic equality between the minor artisans and merchants and the rich 'international' businessmen. The twenty-one 'arts' should in future take part in communal functions from which the rich 'rentiers' would be excluded. Once again, the majority of the artisans were rebelling against the political monopoly enjoyed by the rich businessmen and the fact that they controlled many of the guilds. It should be noted that, as a short time previously under Walter of Brienne, the creating of three extra guilds was demanded, of which one would be for the *ciompi*, so that they could at last be assured of some of the protection afforded by institutionalized solidarity. There was nothing new in that nor, in itself, anything insurrectional. But some conspirators had been preparing for a rebellion: the following day, 9 July, the unrest was at its height in the working-class districts; it was led by artisans of whom one, at least, was undoubtedly very rich. Now one of the conspirators, after his arrest, was to be interrogated under torture. So on 20 July, thousands of rioters besieged the palace of the signoria to demand the release of this conspirator, Simoncino. The only protection for the men inside was given by the militiamen of the few districts which had remained faithful to the authorities, supported by reinforcements from the *contado*. But this was not enough and, during the night, members of the minor 'arts' and the *ciompi,* who had formed an alliance and even worked out a common programme, set fire to patrician palaces.

The common programme was set before the priors on 22 July after another day of pillaging and burning; the woollen 'art', legal archives and – significantly – *fiscal* archives having been the major targets. There was nothing really new in the terms of this common programme, which called for the reinstatement of outlaws, a general amnesty to cover those involved in the disturbances, the setting up of an 'art' for the *popolo minuto* which would include men previously excluded from the organization of the 'arts', and the ending of prison sentences for debtors. Crowds blocked the Palazzo Vecchio from which the priors must have escaped before it was invaded by the rioters. At the head of the rioters was a wool-carder, Michele di Lando, who had himself elected the new gonfalonier of justice. Power had fallen into the hands of the insurgents.

How did the victors use their victory? There was a curious mixture of reforms in favour of the lower strata and a festive atmosphere ('festive' in its truest ethnological sense). The new *Balia* was made up of representatives from all the 'arts', including the three new ones for the *minuti* (the twenty-fourth being reserved for the *ciompi*). It should be made clear that, as far as the 'arts' which were already represented were concerned, all men belonging to families in power before the revolt were expelled. . . in favour, sometimes, of families which were powerful but in league with the rioters. Sixty 'knights of the people' were created; first and foremost among them, it goes without saying, Salvestro de' Medici, whose influence was still very great. Were they trying to make a laughing-stock of noble customs? To believe that would probably be to go against our experience of history.

Was the union between the *ciompi* and the artisans of the minor 'arts' going to last? In effect, the artisans, whether they were well-off or not, wanted a return to order as economic activity, which had fallen very low since the start of the troubles, needed revitalizing. On the one hand, there were more searches carried out in order to disarm the city-dwellers; on the other, there were attempts to re-open all the workshops and all those shops which were still closed. But many stayed closed, and this led to acute unemployment. Food supplies also met with some difficulty. However, the main discontent was political in nature. Instead of carrying on with the expected reforms, the *Balia* attended to the most urgent things first by ordering a compulsory loan – since the coffers were empty – which was supposed to hit only at the rich taxpayers, but which caused the rest some anxiety nevertheless. It was decided that the vote would be limited to certain taxpayers: out of some 13,000 members of the three new 'arts' only a sixth were declared eligible . . .. Basically, and despite appearances, the newcomers in the government were not the poor, but relatively well-off people, small merchants and heads of small businesses (the *ciompi* themselves, one ought to note, were not all impoverished).

The result was a deep discontent among the extremists, who did not accept a government controlled by clienteles of the Medici, Strozzi or Scali, hence the 'radicalization' of a group of the rebels, who had perhaps become more sensitive to latent millenarian aspirations in Florence. The *Popolo di Dio*, composed of members of the lower strata (especially wool-carders, who were the most active), looked on those of their own people who took part in government as traitors. At the head of the *Popolo di Dio* were the 'Eight Saints of the Popolo di Dio'. The *Balia* was reminded of those demands which it had not satisfied. It was then that Michele di Lando stood up against his former friends and, on 31 August, the new revolt failed and the day ended in a manhunt.

Why did it fail? Who was responsible? Was it the common people who seem to have abandoned the 'rabble'? To a certain extent. Was it the property owners? But there had been some of these amongst the rioters, particularly butchers (as always at that time). Might it not have been, too, that the *ciompi*, far from having any feeling of 'class consciousness', were in no way a homogeneous group (there were well-to-do men amongst them), and that their interests, which were sometimes conflicting, were only apparently protected by ambitious men who dreamed of making a career for themselves in government? Were the troops betrayed by their leaders? Perhaps, and sooner than they thought: certain rebel leaders were later to rise in the social hierarchy and make money in Florence or other cities. One such was Michele di Lando. As for the businessmen involved in the revolt (there was a member of the Strozzi family, for example), they plotted and schemed, sometimes from the outside, in the most classical and most established traditions of Italy.

Like so many others, the *ciompi* may well have been no more than a tactical force exploited by others. It was small comfort to know that Salvestro de' Medici and even Michele di Lando were exiled, when the reaction, which was to last several years, suppressed the twenty-fourth, then the twenty-second and twenty-third, 'art'. And the overriding fear that such disorder might recur consolidated the position of the oligarchy which had returned to power. It was the Medici, half a century later, who were to bridle this oligarchy.

The troubles in France in 1379–1383 began with a disturbance in Paris, which arose out of an apparently trivial incident to do with rights of precedence during Charles V's funeral on 24 September 1380. The affair is significant, for the unrest, which was to recur (and often in a much more intensive form), was bound up with the change of sovereign. And this same conjunction of events is to be found several times right up to the early modern period: each authoritarian reign – the reign of the 'wise king', which had just ended, had been such – would be followed by a 'natural *détente*' leading, when the new king was still very young, at best to irresolute government, at worst to a period of restlessness and revolts. The causes thus tended to be chiefly political and due to the strengthening of the state's power. They were also frequently linked with fiscality itself. This is quite clear in the events of 1380–1383, if one sets aside the Flemish case (see below): people took advantage not just of the difficulties which went with Charles VI's youth, but also of a wish made on his death-bed by Charles V who, contrary to custom, seems to have wanted to tie the hands of his successor by stopping the aids. The French tax-payers, who were not yet fully aware of the 'definitive' nature of the taxes, thought themselves free and, without waiting any longer, they called for a tax strike. The Parisians held a demonstration in front of the royal palace on 14 November 1380 and demanded the effective abolition of the aids. It was an anti-fiscal demonstration, but it was also anti-semitic: anti-Jewish disturbances, in France as in Spain (where they were much more serious), in future went hand in hand with almost all forms of urban unrest, the fashion having been set by the chiliastic movements.

The beginning of 1382 was particularly disturbed, especially in Rouen and Paris. Taxation is all the more difficult for the ordinary people to bear while a long economic depression lingers on. Now an ordinance was put out on 15 January concerning the levying of new aids. By February, officers had fixed the amount for Normandy; so on 24 February the *Harelle* (from *haro*, a form of judicial protest in Norman law) broke out in Rouen. Artisans from the textile industry gathered together, the prison gates were opened and pillaging went on for three days, while the insurgents attacked royal officers (naturally), rich burghers, clerics and also Jews. Was this anti-fiscal riot hostile to seignorial rights (title-deeds were burnt only in the Saint-Ouen monastery) and to the rich in general?

This is not very likely. Although some lords and rich merchants had their possessions seized, there were others who sided with the rioters: for example, "some rich merchants and vintners supported the riot", wrote one contemporary. Looking towards the past, the revolt, under the influence of the rebel craftsmen, called for a return to the privileges of the *charte aux Normands.*

The monarchy did not react immediately: on his way to Rouen on 1 March, Charles VI turned back when he heard of the disturbances involving the *Maillotins* in Paris. Through the Italian, Buonaccorso Pitti, we have an impartial account of what, at the start, was no more than a regrettable incident which took place on the populous Right Bank in Paris. A fiscal agent, in his attempts to collect the tax on fruit and vegetables, tried to seize the produce of a small stallholder. She shouted: "Down with taxes!", whereupon a crowd assembled; they rushed to the collectors' houses, which they pillaged, killing the collectors themselves. A search for weapons began. Now, at the new Châtelet, du Guesclin had had 3,000 leaden mallets stored because of the war against the English: the crowds broke down the gates and seized these mallets (*maillets*) which gave the revolt its name. Then the pillaging of dwellings belonging to the king's officers grew worse. And, in their turn, burghers armed themselves: they joined the rebels – "through fear of the common people", some would claim. . . – and a few nobles joined them, too. The entire Right Bank was soon in the hands of the insurgents; members of the government went to find the king who had taken refuge at Vincennes. During the first fortnight in March, acts of pillaging and murders (about thirty in all – sixteen victims were Jews – as against only two in Rouen) followed one another without respite.

If the revolt of the *Maillotins* was more violent than the *Harelle,* one of the principal reasons lies in the greater number of marginals in the capital, especially the unemployed and labourers without fixed employment because of the depression in trade. The first demonstrators, the cloth-shearers, the curriers, the road-diggers and so on, the rustics who had taken refuge in Paris after the trials of the war, had soon been joined by "very young idlers" – probably young people out of work – and particularly by "people of strange occupation", vagabonds and *caïmans* (= criminals). In Paris, more so than Rouen, the *commonalty* was overrun by these marginals.

The monarchy seemed to give way at first by having prisoners released. However, this did not stop the mob from pillaging the Châtelet, and the revolt found new strength. But repression was not far off. Certainly, apparent concessions were made, with promises of a return to the old tax system, the one which had been in force in St Louis' reign, the customary reference point of the malcontents. Yet, with the support of all those citizens who were weary of disorder (or who wanted to dissociate themselves from the marginals who had become too much of an encumbrance), the king's uncles had twenty or so executions carried out to serve as a warning. Then, on 29 March, the court entered Rouen as if it were a conquered city: an amnesty was granted only after a dozen people had been put to death, all arms had been given up, a heavy fine had been paid and the privilege of the commune had been abolished.

Things were not over. In the first place, tax resistance had reached all the Norman towns, Amiens, Orleans, some towns in Champagne, and even Lyons. Moreover, the unrest was fanned by the choosing of delegates for the Estates General which were to meet at Compiègne, and which were naturally going to protest against the levying of the aids. But it was another, more distant, revolt which did more than anything to sustain the unrest, namely, the Ghent rebellion, which had begun in 1379. In one sense, this had started off as a conflict between Ghent and Bruges: in 1379 Louis de Male, the count of Flanders, had authorized the digging of a canal between the River Lys and Bruges, thereby posing a threat to Ghent's trade. The diggers were soon attacked by Ghent boatmen and weavers, who even killed the bailiff. The unrest gradually reached the weavers of Bruges and Ypres. By the Autumn of 1379 almost the entire region had risen, and peasants were being recruited into the rebels' army; the privileges of the patriciate, the *poorters,* came under attack and restoration of 'communal freedoms' was demanded. We know that the leader, who did much for the cohesion of the revolt, was Philip van Artevelde. Was the affair above all a question of opposition between *commonalty* and upper bourgeoisie? If that was the case, the opposition was political rather than social. But, more than this, it was the struggle of a town against the comital state of Flanders, the struggle of a town which wanted to control the surrounding countryside, like the *contados* held by the large Italian cities. Philip even took the title of *ruwaert* (= governor) and he carried on negotiations with the king of England as if he really were the lord of Flanders. All this was extremely disturbing to Charles VI's uncles, all the more so since news from Flanders was fanning the flames of unrest in Paris and Rouen. Ghent's great victory on 3 May 1382 (Count Louis de Male only just escaped capture) served to encourage firstly the people of Rouen, who, at the beginning of August, put to flight the officers of the aids, and subsequently the people of Paris. A new type of *co-juratio* was formed in the capital: the sworn associates, amongst whom there were some cloth manufacturers, promised (on an oath taken on mallets) to co-operate in the rejection of taxation, undertaking to go as far as insurrection and the murder of the provost of the merchants. There was secret correspondence with Ghent.

Philip the Bold and his brothers had wind of the conspiracy, but they had to mark time in Paris until the Flemish rebellion had been crushed. In response to Louis de Male's appeal, they organized an expedition in August: on 27 November, at Roosebeke to the south of Bruges, the French chivalry defeated the majority of the insurgents and Philip van Artevelde perished in the mêlée. The 1302 defeat of the Golden Spurs was handsomely avenged. To be sure, Ghent was going to resist for some years yet (no one dared besiege it during this campaign nor during subsequent ones), but the rebellion in the rest of Flanders had failed: Philip the Bold was soon to become count of Flanders, a count whose power commanded great respect. Thus, after Roosebeke, Philip and his brothers could turn back to Paris and crush the capital. The repression, definitive this time, began in January 1383. The tribunals spent more than a month sentencing the main leaders, including men like Jean des Mares, an attorney in the *Parlement* (though from a milieu loyal to the Valois), who was reproached for his recent demagogy and who was not saved by the attempts at conciliation he had made the year before. Even extremely old scores were settled: one of the men behind the killing of the marshals on 28 February 1358, Nicolas le Flament, was executed . . .. And the capital lost its provostship of the merchants, although it had not been insubordinate as it had been in 1358: the government of the uncles, because it felt more insecure, was also more merciless than the regent who, a quarter of a century earlier, had granted a general amnesty and had not abolished this office. For some time after 1383, royal authority gained ground, that is until the king went mad, or indeed until the outbreak of the fratricidal struggles between the Armagnacs and Burgundians.

The third seat of unrest, in the Empire, was very different. In the Hanse towns, which had remained quiet during the preceding period (above, p. 120), there were outbreaks of trouble in places from as early as 1374. Lübeck suffered particularly, where the most serious disturbances occurred from 1380. The revolts were due to burdensome taxation, and in this respect the movements were certainly bound up with circumstances. But, it was also a question of craft-guilds – the butchers readily taking the lead – attempting to accede to the rank of a new elite (attempts which were successful ultimately only in Brunswick and Cologne). These rebellions were thus of a mixed nature, and they could just as well have found a place in the previous chapter.

At a date which varied from one economic sector to another and from one region to another, the long depression was to give way to a new phase of expansion (phase A) in the course of the fifteenth century, around 1450 in northern areas, probably earlier in the south. The result was a substantial easing of difficulties in both town and country. Wars were ending or becoming rarer, the danger of epidemics was fading, and the population was on the increase once again. There were still going to be disturbances, such as those in France towards the end of Charles VII's reign or those which Louis XI had to face in 1465. But it would rarely be a question of *popular* rebellions, and they would not provoke serious destruction. Some towns in the Low Countries were to suffer on account of the struggle between the king of France and Charles the Bold, but these were predominantly *political* revolts.

From 1450, in particular, there were thus virtually no more disturbances which could be attributed to depressed circumstances. In towns where relations between certain masters and their journeymen were not always at their best, the journeymen felt their lot was more bearable as unemployment declined and the economy improved. Except in regions of England where the enclosure system prevailed and southern regions where farmers had to endure the presence of shepherds, the peasantry enjoyed a better life: produce sold better, including corn from 1480 to 1490. And despite the growth in the population, the famine of around 1500 would threaten only a very few areas.

But the prime cause of the decrease in rebellions linked to critical circumstances lies perhaps elsewhere. Taxation remained heavy, indeed was often heavier. At first, people found it easier to pay the taxes since they earned more. More particularly, the question no longer arose of contesting the principle of taxation or its actual levying because, almost everywhere, the state was growing stronger. There was no power vacuum at the close of the Middle Ages which might have encouraged would-be rebels, not even in England (at least after the Wars of the Roses) and certainly not in Spain, of course, where unification was reaching completion, France or Italy. The authoritarian monarchies of Charles VII and Louis XI knew how to command obedience. Like other monarchies, moreover, they were taking more interest in economic matters: pre-mercantilism was born. And, like the dukes of Burgundy, they knew how to control the towns. This was to the decided benefit of the ordinary people and those who aspired to the rank of elite, and to the detriment of the oligarchies. Italy was following a similar path: the age of personal lordships had arrived, as in Florence, for example, where in 1434 Cosimo de' Medici assumed effective power to the delight of the increasing number of opponents of the oligarchic regime of the *grassi*.

For the time being at least, the renewed power of the state was considered a relative good by the strata composed of the common people; these latter were no longer willing, or able, to allow themselves to be used so much by elites or marginals as participants in would-be revolts. The exception was in Germany where the Peasants' War could be dimly seen on the horizon – perhaps because that particular country stayed more fragmented and more anarchical than Italy.

Conclusion

Since not much pioneer work has been done in this field for the Middle Ages, the part entitled 'Approaches to the problem' has had to take up half this book: in it, a number of theoretical problems were considered, although those arising from psychoanalytical phenomena, crowd psychology and so on were not really given their due – partly because of insufficient material put forward by medievalists. Through lack of space, the 'Typology' part has not been able to deal with every revolt, but those omitted could be placed within our classification, which enjoys the flexibility of an open synthesis. Here is some proof. At the close of the Middle Ages, Scandinavia, like Western Europe proper, witnessed many peasant disturbances. These were certainly linked to a depression, a depression which was very similar to that examined in the last chapter and which gave rise to fairly similar social effects. Thus, when the Danes defeated an army of rustics near Visby on the island of Gotland in 1361, they overcame men who had been moved to rebellion by political and fiscal motives. For taxation was even further advanced in Scandinavia than in other countries, with the exception of England: as early as 1280 the Swedes were unhappy about the fiscal privileges of the nobles . . .. One could say that, from Norway to Finland, the rustics, who had a keener sense of independence than their contemporaries further south, saw taxation as their chief enemy. Hence the frequency of rural troubles at the end of the Middle Ages, as in the sixteenth century.

One could liken these troubles to the 1358 Jacquerie since they, too, were fairly frequently anti-nobiliary, being against seignorial dues. But the reason behind this recalls the 'universality' of the strength of the feudal bond between tenants and lords: if the people rose not only against the state and its fisc but also against lords, it was because it was often a question of *new* lords with whom the people felt no bond, as they did with the old ones (Cl. Nordmann). Thus the social history of a country as far away as Scandinavia in no way conflicts with the 'Typology' which we here propose and which it would be easy to refine without brutal modification.

But our attempt at a typology has not allowed us to trace a single development spanning the whole period. This carries with it the inevitable shortcoming of not giving enough importance to the strong and weak phases of disturbances. The Scandinavian example nevertheless reminds us of the exceptional number of rebellions which occurred at the end of the Middle Ages. Why not go back to the Saint-Simonian distinction ('rediscovered' in turn by Comte, Marx even, Nietzsche, Durkheim, etc.) between *organic periods* and *critical periods,* on condition that in its application to the Middle Ages it should be slightly modified? For to Durkheim, amongst others, a critical period is a "period of transition when the entire species [it is a question of some given social species] is in the process of evolving and has not become definitively fixed in its new form", thus a period of relaxing of social bonds, of *social mutability* (Monnerot), heralding fundamental transformations. In this sense – an extreme one – it would be difficult to detect such a critical phase in the Middle Ages: the medieval millennium seems to have been entirely an organic period since, in the societies of the time, by virtue of membership of the Church, there existed a common measure for all individuals, except, once again, for the marginals. But one could easily interpret the term *critical period* as simply indicating a particularly fertile period for disturbances.

Thus, with Comte, one could maintain that the 1300s saw the end of an organic period and the start of a critical period, that is a period of upswing for revolts which was going to end only in the course of the fifteenth century (for example, in France) – that is, when it did not last into the middle of the sixteenth century (as, for example, in Germany and Scandinavia). If one followed Durkheim, for whom social and religious cohesion go hand in hand, one could say, it is true, that other countries like France saw this critical phase extend into the sixteenth century in the form of religious conflicts. Further evidence is found if one turns to Nietzsche, for example, according to whom it is during critical periods that great personalities come to the fore – for, in the years before 1500 and during the Renaissance, many such individuals were to appear. But let us not exaggerate: the preceding organic phase had also seen the birth of many great personalities . . . .

It is because we do not discern any 'social dissolution', even at the end of the Middle Ages, that we have largely avoided using the term *mass* (not just because the number of participants in many revolts is open to doubt): the day of the masses will come only with the destruction of the societies of orders. Before then, the masses did not really exist, for individuals still had well-defined stations and had not yet been 'equalised' by a destitution more moral than material. On the other hand, but this is different, we have suggested the idea of masses in talking of a manipulated tactical force – a concept which calls for further research.

As far as history is able to throw light on rebellions, it will have to take serious account of Marx's warning about what is generally known as class prejudice (in our terminology, group prejudice). Amongst chroniclers, this emerges in what they say and what they suppress (for example, who won or lost such and such a revolt in the end?), what they gloss over or alter. Such a pitfall makes all the more valuable research concentrated on less striking, but more reliable sources, as has recently been done for the Florentine revolt of 1378. Historical criticism is particularly tricky in these matters.

Bibliography

In this bibliography we include only the most important and convenient works, most of which have their own bibliography.

Alphandéry P., and Dupront A., *La Chrétienté et l'idée de croisade, 2 vols.,* Michel A., Paris, 1954 and 1959.

Ansart P., *Sociologie de Saint-Simon,* Presses Universitaires de France, Paris, 1970; *Saint-Simon* (texts), the same, 1969.

Arbousse-Bastide P., *Auguste Comte* (texts), Presses Universitaires de France, Paris, 1968.

Arnaud P., *Sociologie de Comte,* Presses Universitaires de France, Paris, 1969.

Aron, R., *Marxismes imaginaires,* N.R.F., Paris, 1970.

Baechler J., *Les phénomènes révolutionnaires,* Presses Universitaires de France, Paris, 1970; *Les origines du capitalisme,* N.R.F., Paris, 1971.

Caillois R., *Le mythe et l'homme,* Gallimard, Paris, 1938; *L'homme et le sacré,* Gallimard, Paris, 1963.

Camus A., *L'homme révolté,* Gallimard, Paris, 1951.

Cohn N., *The pursuit of the Millennium: revolutionary millenarians and mystical anarchists of the Middle Ages,* revised and expanded edition, Temple Smith, London, 1970.

Cornu R. and Lagneau J., *Hiérarchies et classes sociales,* Colin A., Paris, 1969.

Dahrendorf R., *Class and class conflict in industrial society,* Stanford Univ. Press, Stanford, 1959.

Decouflé A., *Sociologie des révolutions,* Presses Universitaires de France, Paris, 1970.

De Roover R., *La pensée économique des scolastiques,* Institut d'Etudes médiévales, Montreal, 1971.

Dingemans G., *Psychanalyse des peuples et des civilisations; tragédie du passé, angoisse du présent, espoir d'avenir,* Colin A., Paris, 1971.

Dobson R. B., *The Peasants' Revolt of 1381,* Macmillan, London, 1970.

Duby G., *L'An Mil,* Julliard, Paris, 1967; *Des sociétés médiévales,* Gallimard, Paris, 1971.

Eliade M., *Myth and reality,* translated by Trask, W. R. from *Aspects du mythe,* Allen and Unwin, London, 1964; *Cosmos and history,* translated by Trask, W. R. from *Le mythe de l'éternel retour,* Harper Torchbooks, New York, 1959.

Ellul J., *Autopsie de la révolution,* Calmann-Lévy, Paris, 1969.

Engels F., *The German Revolutions,* edited and with an introduction by Krieger L., Univ. of Chicago Press, Chicago and London, 1967.

Fédou R., *L'Etat au Moyen Age,* Presses Universitaires de France, Paris, 1971.

Fourquin G., *Histoire économique de l'Occident médiéval,* 2nd edn, Colin A., Paris, 1971; *Seigneurie et féodalité au Moyen Age,* Presses Universitaires de France, Paris, 1970; *La France rurale des grandes migrations à 1328* (in *Histoire de la France rurale,* vol. 1, ed. Duby G., Le Seuil, Paris, 1975).

Freud S., *Civilization and its discontents,* translated by Joan Riviere, Hogarth Press, London, 1930.

Gérard, A., *La Révolution française, mythes et interprétations, 1789–1970,* Flammarion, Paris, 1970.

Guenée B., *L'Occident aux quatorzième et quinzième siècles, les Etats,* Presses Universitaires de France, Paris, 1971.

Hérésies et Sociétés dans l'Europe pré-industrielle (onzième-dix-huitième siècles), Mouton, Paris and the Hague, 1968.

Heers J., *L'Occident aux XIVe et XVe siècles; aspects économiques et sociaux,* 4th edn, Presses Universitaires de France, Paris, 1973; *Le clan familial au moyen âge,* Presses Universitaires de France, Paris, 1974. (English translation to be published shortly.)

Hilton R., *Bond men made free; medieval peasant movements and the English Rising of 1381,* Temple Smith, London, 1973.

Lacroix J., *La sociologie d'Auguste Comte,* Presses Universitaires de France, Paris, 1967.

Laubier J., *Auguste Comte; sociologie* (texts), Presses Universitaires de France, Paris, 1969.

Les libertés urbaines et rurales du onzième au quatorzième siècle, "Pro Civitate", Brussels, 1968.

Marx K. and Engels F., *The German Ideology,* translated by Ryazanskaya, S., Lawrence and Wishart, London, 1965; *The Communist Manifesto,* Centenary edition, Communist Party, London, 1948.

Mollat M. and Wolff Ph., *Ongles bleus, Jacques et Ciompi,* Calmann-Lévy, Paris, 1970.

Monnerot J., *Sociologie du communisme,* 7th edn, (the 1st was in 1949) Paris, N.R.F.; *Sociologie de la révolution,* Fayard, Paris, 1968.

Mousnier R., *Fureurs paysannes,* Calmann-Lévy, Paris, 1967; *Problèmes de stratification sociale,* Presses Universitaires de France, Paris, 1968; *Les hiérarchies sociales de 1450 à nos jours,* Presses Universitaires de France, Paris, 1969; *La plume, la faucille et le marteau,* the same, 1970.

Newcomb T. M., Turner R. A. and Converse P. E., *Social psychology: the study of human interaction,* Holt, Rinehart and Winston, New York, 1965.

Paillet M., *Marx contre Marx. La société technobureaucratique,* Denoël, Paris, 1971.

Perrin G., *Sociologie de Pareto,* Presses Universitaires de France, Paris, 1966.

Petit-Dutaillis C., *Les communes françaises,* Michel A., Paris, 1947. (English translation to be published shortly.)

Renouard Y., *Histoire de Florence,* Presses Universitaires de France, Paris, 1967; *Les villes d'Italie de la fin du dixième siècle au début du quatorzième siècle,* new edition, SEDES, Paris, 1969.

Rocher G., *Introduction à la sociologie générale,* 3 vols., H.M.H., Paris, 1970.

Rubinstein, N., *Florentine studies,* Faber and Faber, London, 1968.

Souyri P., *Le marxisme après Marx,* Flammarion, Paris, 1970.

Sur le féodalisme, Editions Sociales, "CERM", Paris, 1971.

Tchakhotine S., *Le viol des foules par la propagande politique,* new edn, Gallimard, Paris, 1968.

Index

Flanders, 60, 65, 71, 72, 76, 78, 85, 89, 90, 112, 113, 117, 118, 133–4, 143, 149, 155, 157, 158
Florence, 57, 62, 64, 70, 71, 74, 77, 116, 122, 123, 133, 150, 151, 154, 160, 163
Frankfurt, 94, 98
Frederick I, Barbarossa, 93
Frederick II, 9, 93, 94, 95, 96, 97, 98
French Revolution (1789), xii, 12, 13, 29, 69, 110, 124, 127, 132, 136, 140, 142, 144
Freud, 10
Fribourg, 120
Froissart, 73, 76, 101, 136, 137, 142

Génicot, L., 49
Genoa, 64, 114, 121
Ghent, 74, 118, 119, 157, 158
Ghibellines, 95, 115, 121, 152
Girondists, 124
Glaber, Raoul, 84
Gotland, 161
Gregory VII, pope, 72
Grimaldi family, 121
Guelphs, 95, 115, 121, 123, 152
Guérins, 126
Guesclin, du, 156
Guizot, 29

Haguenau, 120
Hainaut, 90
Halle, 93
Ham, 111
Hanse towns, 65, 120, 158
Harelle, 155, 156
Hebrews, 5, 6
Hegel, 29, 30, 31, 91
Heraclitus, 30, 31
Hitler, 73
Hobbes, xi
Hundred Years War, 36, 46, 48, 56, 118, 128, 132, 149

Lactantius, 7
Lando, Michele di, 71, 153, 154
Laon, 77, 111, 112, 125
le Bel, Jean, 135, 137
le Coq, Robert, 77, 125
le Flament, Nicolas, 158
Legoix, 126
Leliaerts, 117, 118
Le Mans, 111
le Muisi, Gilles, 119
Le Neubourg, 146
Lenin, 30
Lessing, 91
Liège, 113, 118
Lille, 90, 104
Lipan, 106
Litster, Geoffrey, 76
London, 101, 142, 143
Longjumeau, 136
Louis VI, king of France, 35
Louis VIII, king of France, xiii, 90
Louis XI, king of France, 50, 128, 159
Louis XVI, king of France, 127
Louis XVIII, king of France, 110
Louis of Orleans, 127
Louis the Pious, 41
Louvre assembly, 46
Loyseau, 46, 51, 58
Lübeck, 94, 158
Lucca, 115
Luce, Siméon, 76
Luchaire, A., 110
Lucian, 99
Luther, xiii, 98, 148
Lyons, 7, 22, 106, 157

Machiavelli, xi, 4
Magdeburg, 120